f769.5
K63
1974   Klamkin   150
ART   Picture postcards
                c. 1

Picture Postcards

Books by Marian Klamkin

Flower Arranging for Period Decoration
Flower Arrangements That Last
White House China
American Patriotic and Political China
The Collector's Book of Art Nouveau
The Collector's Book of Bottles
The Collector's Book of Boxes
The Collector's Book of Wedgwood
Hands To Work: Shaker Folk Art and Industries
The Collector's Guide to Depression Glass
Picture Postcards

PICTURE POSTCARDS

Marian Klamkin

**Illustrated with photographs
by Charles Klamkin**

DODD, MEAD & COMPANY

NEW YORK

First published in the United States in 1974
ISBN 0-396-06889-8
Library of Congress Catalog Card Number: 73-15063
Printed in Great Britain

Contents

1

Introduction

A popular graffito among today's youth is 'Nostalgia isn't what it used to be' and it is probably a reaction of youth to the current craze for objects and information of bygone days. Things to which some of us have a great deal of trouble relating have become extremely important to others. We search for and collect many objects that tell us something about our past history, our social habits, the disappearing scenery that was once so familiar and our methods of communicating with one another. For all these reasons, and others, picture postcards are rapidly becoming an important category in the vast field of nostalgic collectibles.

Many types of ephemeral paper objects are eagerly sought by collectors today, but picture postcard collectors are in a category by themselves. For these collector-historians there is an endless variety from which to choose and hundreds of categories in which they may specialise. Picture postcards are easy to store, take up little space in today's crowded houses and apartments, are still not exhorbitantly expensive as compared to other collectible objects, are not breakable, can usually be found in decent condition and can offer many hours of constructive enjoyment and instruction.

Unlike many categories of collectible objects, the hobby of picture postcard collecting is enjoying a popularity for a second time. Picture postcards, those of the period between 1880 and 1918, were originally published to appeal to collectors and were manufactured as collectors' items when they were new. Therefore, there is a great deal of early literature concerning what was made, who the artists were who designed them and less about the publishers who issued them. These collectors' newsletters and magazines, published at the beginning of this century when postcard collecting was the most popular hobby in England and America, are now eagerly sought for the information they can offer to today's collectors. There are many newsletters currently being published in both countries that attempt to serve a similar purpose for the modern collectors of old picture postcards.

While many of the earliest have already reached the established category of 'antiques' and are almost a hundred years old, many other later cards are just as desirable to collectors for a variety of reasons although they have some time to go before they can be considered bona fide antiques. However, in the category of collectible paper objects age is not as important in establishing value as are some other criteria.

Although millions of picture postcards were published between 1880 and the end of World War I, not that many have survived and certain desirable ones are not as easy to find as one might think. While few were published in limited editions, there were some rather special postcards that were made in small quantities

to appeal to the elite collectors who gathered for their albums only those cards thought to be the 'most artistic' and these are still the most sought after by modern collectors.

Randall Rhoades of Ashland, Ohio, coined a word in the early 1930s that became the accepted description of the study of picture postcards. 'Deltiology', taken from the Greek word, *deltion*, meaning a small picture or card and *logos*, meaning a science or knowledge, is now used widely as the one word to cover the vast area of postcard study. A 'deltiophile' is a collector of picture postcards and 'deltiography' is the making of postcards. A 'deltiologist' is one who is interested in the history of the postcard and

Ocean views were popular with collectors prior to World War I.

8

Copies of great art masterpieces have been made continuously.

helps to add to the information concerning the subject. The leading American organisation for the dissemination of information on the collecting and history of postcards is called 'Deltiologists of America'.

Within the past few years deltiology has become one of the fastest growing collecting hobbies in England and America. The cards collected and studied include the earliest issued by the postal services of both countries to the most absurd comic cards of the first part of this century. The hobby is quickly approaching the proportions of coin and stamp collecting to which it is somewhat related.

There is a category of interest to almost every deltiologist. Early transportation, communication, subjects of geographic interest, work of a particular publisher or artist, illustrations of children, toys and dolls, religious, patriotic or political subjects, American Indians, Scottish tartans, performing arts; the list of categories is almost inexhaustible. A lot was happening in the world of art and science at the close of the last century and the beginning of this one. It's all recorded on the small printed cards that were sold by the millions when they were new.

The events, prejudices and attitudes of Edwardian England and turn-of-the-century America can be found on the three-and-a-half by five-and-a-half inch cards that one could purchase for a penny on either side of the ocean and that could be mailed across that ocean for the price of a twopenny stamp. While the prejudices of the period might have been slightly different in the two countries during that exciting period, they were clear-cut and easily expressed by political cartoonists and collectors sought cards that expressed their attitudes towards many controversial subjects of the time. American cards that were popular depicted cartoon versions of black children that had verses written in dialect. These are now collected as examples of the frightening, but accepted, manner in which blacks were treated. At the same time hen-pecked husbands seem to have been a subject of great mirth in England. Purported 'membership' in organisations that, fortunately, did not exist were sent by postcard to any friends thought to have a good enough sense of humor not to have been hurt by the all-too-obvious messages. Drunks were the subject of many cards that were often sent out as humorous New Year's Day greetings. The town drunk was, at the turn of the century, more to be laughed at than pitied. Mothers-in-law were also considered proper subjects for ridicule.

Subjects of love as well as hate were used in the 'golden age'. Even proposals of marriage were printed and ready to send for a penny if the sender felt unable to pop the question in a more socially acceptable manner. Valentine postcards were extremely popular and Leap Year was the cause for many thousands of ladies to send their own forms of proposal on the one day in four years when it was their prerogative.

There is, perhaps, no better record of the costumes of any period of the past than one can find on the photographic and artistic postcards of the Edwardian period, which show the obvious change from corseted restrictive women's clothing to the freer dress of the early twentieth century. The enormous hats, made to balance the narrow-hemmed dresses that were fashionable, are documented in many forms on postcard ladies. The period when women were finally beginning to strain at the submissive role they had been playing, and suffragettes, out

9

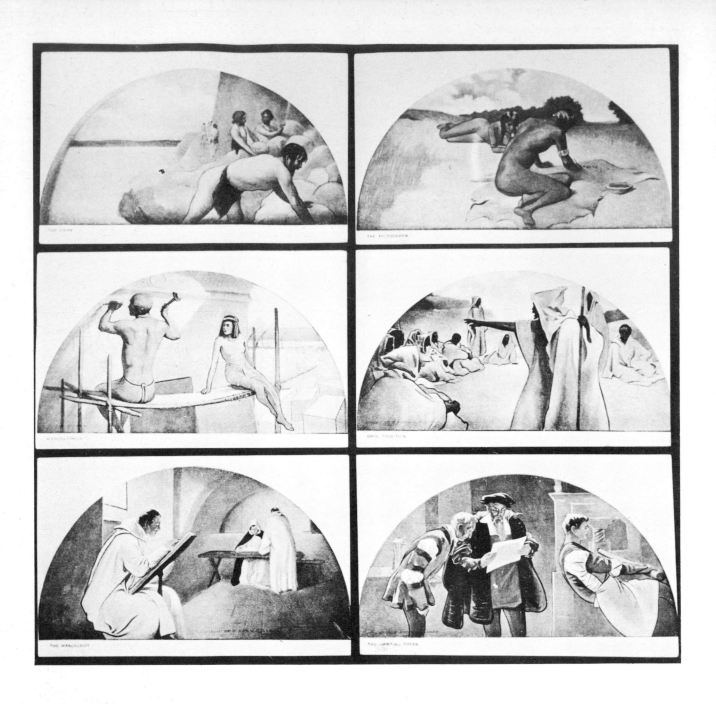

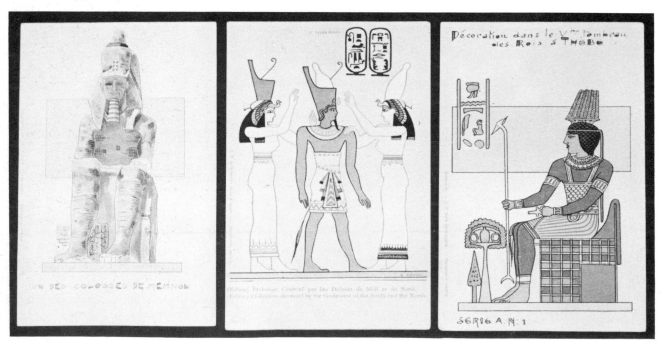

10

Opposite, left. The story of the development of communications is told.

Below. Picture postcards were made almost everywhere in the world. The more exotic, the better for collectors.

39322 Dr. Frederick A. Cook, Arctic Explorer, in his Arctic costume, and the Steamer Bradley, which bore him upon his successful search for the North Pole, which he discovered April 21, 1908.

39319 Lieut. Robert E. Peary, Arctic Explorer, and the Steamer Roosevelt used by him in his last dash to the North Pole, which he discovered on April 6, 1909.

Right. Feats of daring and the men who performed them were all recorded.

Below. Main streets and famous landmarks were all subjects for album cards.

St. Peter Street, St. Paul, Minn.

111 Copyright 1908 by Paul Reichelt.

First Lake; Fulton Chain; Adirondack Mountains.

"Sugar Loaf Mt." Hudson River Highlands on the Str.

ROSEDALE

View up Hudson River from Sea Coast Battery, West Point.

DANBURY CONN. Danbury Fair, looking North.

Seaside Park, Showing Locomobile Co. of America, BRIDGEPORT, Conn.

marching to achieve equal rights with men in their choice of government, were documented from both a negative and a positive viewpoint.

The period between 1880 and 1918 was one of swift social and scientific changes and these are all recorded on picture postcards of the era. The invention of the electric light, the general use of the telephone (about to make postal cards as a means of fast communication as archaic as the pony express), the experimentation with all sorts of airborne machinery, and the improvement of earth-bound transportation are all depicted and many collectors specialise in one or all of these fascinating categories. Many of these cards are amusing today, but were taken very seriously when they were first printed. Especially funny to us today are the attempts to glamorise and romanticise the use of the electric light bulb. Today, only the candle flame is supposed to conjure up the proper lighting atmosphere for romantic backgrounds.

Collectors on both sides of the ocean will be able to find views

Hand-colored black and white photography was a technique used on early scenic postcards.

12

20365 Good Tidings

403. ANYTHING FOR ME, MR. POSTMAN?

San Francisco

THE QUICKEST MESSENGER IN LONDON

DISTRICT MESSENGER STARTING FOR CONSTANTINOPLE WITH VALUABLE DOG FOR H.I.M. THE SULTAN.

XMAS MORN. MESSENGER DELIVERING PRESENTS

Postmen and messengers were frequent subjects. Mailman in upper right card is carrying paper pouch that opens up to hold an extra message.

of their hometowns as they looked in the early 1900s. Nineteenth-century buildings that have since been torn down were photographed by local photographers and the pictures sent to Germany where they were printed on postcards and often hand-colored, or otherwise embellished, and sent back for sale in local stores. 'View' cards, those pictures of limited local interest, are still available to deltiologists by the thousands. One may collect picture postcards of a certain town or area and a grouping will show how that place looked sixty or seventy years ago. Some of these view cards are early examples of photography, an art that was in its infancy at the time; many other cards were photographed in black and white and then colored by hand or by lithographic processes.

For art lovers there are many cards that have excellent, although small, reproductions of work of just about every well-known artist who preceded the twentieth century, and many of the contemporary artists who were given places in the world's important museums earned their living designing for postcards

13

or allowing their paintings to be reduced to postcard-size prints.

Some of the artists who designed postcards for a living during the heyday of the collecting craze have become known among today's collectors for the superiority of their work and have recently sprung from anonymity to be in strong demand among knowledgeable deltiologists. Since these minor artists left little other work, details of many of their lives cannot be found by modern researchers. Nevertheless, their styles are well known and they are now as revered in their own genre as many of the important salon artists of the period are in theirs.

While many of the British painters and etchers who enjoyed great popularity for their work at the end of the nineteenth century have faded into oblivion, other artists who concentrated on the bread-and-butter work of designing for Raphael Tuck and other British postcard publishers have achieved a certain kind of immortality among picture postcard enthusiasts. While names like Professor von Weil and Ellen H. Clapsaddle have no meaning to art historians, they are well known and somewhat revered by deltiophiles.

Postcards are collected for other reasons besides their subject matter. In the zeal for creating novelties which would find their way into albums of collectors, many unusual types of materials were used either in the manufacture of the cards themselves or as applied material. Fur, feathers, spangles, glittery sequins, lace, fabric and other bits of appealing materials were applied to post-cards when the subject matter seemed to allow it. All of this required a great deal of handwork and the miracle is that some of these cards were still sold for a penny or two. They are very desirable to today's deltiologists and are treated in a separate chapter.

Postcards were made and sold in such huge quantities during the period leading to World War I that it would be impossible to do more than discuss the major types, the leading publishers and artists and the outstanding items that are collected today. Con-current with the cards, themselves, is the history of some of the subject matter that inspired certain types of designs, and no-where is the history of the Edwardian period better documented pictorially.

German beer and beer halls were favourite subjects of the country that made most of the postcards for the world.

14

2

Collecting Postcards as a Hobby

Famous men and their accomplishments were subjects of thousands of cards.

As collectible items, picture postcards are enormously satisfactory for many reasons. First, they are mostly all the same size and can therefore be easily stored. They are unbreakable, although some must be treated with care in order not to chip coatings or break corners. They can be easily traded or purchased through the mail and most of them can be easily identified by short descriptions. They are artistically pleasing, for we only need collect those that have aesthetic or intellectual appeal for us. There is a lot to be learned by young and old from the study of

many of the postcards that can still be purchased without too large an investment.

For these reasons, and for many others, the hobby of deltiology is once again, after enjoying tremendous popularity during the period preceding World War I, a fast-growing international pastime for thousands of people. Although postcard collecting clubs have flourished in many cities of the world since the 1940s, new groups have organised and many of these publish news bulletins that are available to collectors everywhere. Some of these bulletins are excellent sources for definitive literature on the subject. Certain collectors, with a scholar's bent for careful research, will accumulate check lists of cards representing a particular artist or publisher; others will attempt to trace the origins of some of the more esoteric and unmarked. All of this information is helpful and necessary to deltiologists everywhere and corrections and additions are often volunteered and printed in later issues of newsletters and bulletins.

The completion, or partial completion, of a check list of a

16

SUFFRAGETTE SERIES Nº 2.

ELECTIONEERING

COPYRIGHTED 1909 BY DUNSTON-WEILER LITHOGRAPH CO.

17

A VIEW FROM THE VERANDA. THE BELGRADE. BELGRADE LAKES, MAINE

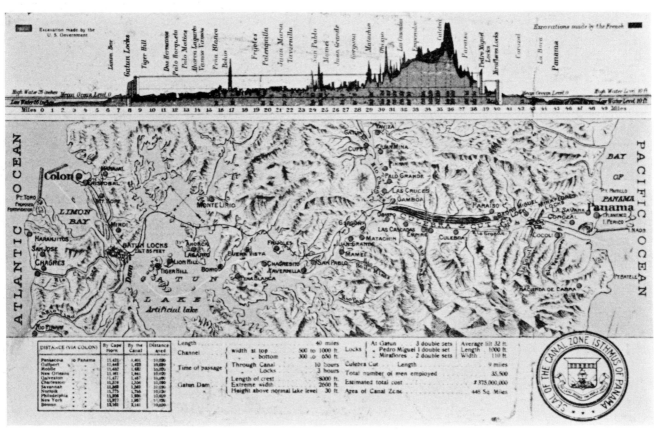

particular artist's work has other ramifications, however. Once the entire signed work is known of an artist's output for postcard design, the prices tend to rise for the cards that are scarce on the list as collectors strive to complete their collections of the work of that artist. Also, for many artists and publishers, especially the more prolific ones, these lists will never be complete. Many cards were unsigned or unmarked. Also, some of the more

Top: no one thought of going on vacation without sending cards home – many were given to clients to help advertise. Above: map card giving statistics of the Panama Canal. Opposite: menu cards were popular with collectors before World War I.

18

Menu

Holidays, with Sauce of Joy
Snow Balls-

Stockings, a la Santa Claus
Festivals,
with Holly and Mistletoe
Gifts, Flavored with Love,

Back-Logs, served whole

Peace and Good-Will
dressed with Charity
Sweet Carols · Good Wishes

May This always be
your
Christmas Menu!

popular designs were pirated by other printers, and where the pirating was done photographically all identifying marks remained as on the original. As the cards have gone out of copyright, some of the most wanted are being reproduced. It is a simple matter for determined forgers to reproduce the work of Ellen Clapsaddle, Frances Brundage and other artists whose work is in demand. Most deltiologists are aware of this and through their handling of many of the old cards would not be fooled into purchasing a reproduction.

Organised collecting has enormous advantages for the deltiologist, for not only information, but postcards, can be exchanged or bought and sold at meetings of the postcard groups. In the United States bourses and exhibits are held at least once a year by most of the postcard clubs and this gives collectors and dealers an opportunity to meet and conduct business in a congenial atmosphere. While some postcard groups keep in touch only through the mail, others have monthly meetings where their collections are discussed and postcards and information are exchanged.

There are several ways of finding out if there is a postcard collecting club or group in one's vicinity. In England one can write to *Postcard World*, 34 Harper House, St. James Crescent, London SW9. This is a publication of the Postcard Collectors Club of Great Britain and a subscription to this periodical should be helpful to collectors anywhere, since many of the same cards

Photographic records of American Indians at the beginning of this century.

20

Lithographic reproductions of paintings of pretty women or handsome landscapes were highly prized for albums.

originally published and sold in Great Britain were exported all over the world. In the United States of America one can write to the International Postcard Collectors Association, Inc., 6380 Wilshire Blvd. Suite 907, Los Angeles, California, 90048. This is the only international collectors club and a membership would be worthwhile for any dedicated deltiologist.

Another method of finding out whether there is already a collectors group organised in one's own community would be to place a small advertisement in one's local newspaper. Most of the large cities in the United States and Great Britain have clubs. If there isn't one already in your community, the advertisement might put you in touch with other collectors who would be willing to organise a group. Many collectors prefer to collect alone, but the advantages of belonging to a group are greater for collectors of postcards than almost any other category of antiques. Most collectors will purchase an entire old postcard album in order to own two or three items that fit into their category of collecting. Other cards hold little or no interest for the specialist-collector, and having collectors of different categories of postcards nearby is often extremely advantageous.

Another advantage of belonging to one or more postcard

Sentimental paintings had a great deal of appeal for postcard collectors at beginning of the century. Because of great volume superb color lithography could be published for pennies.

22

collecting groups is that local dealers advertise in the bulletins issued by the clubs and this puts one in touch with sources that he might otherwise not know about. The bulletins, themselves, are extremely helpful to collectors since this is where the checklists are published. Some of these newsletters and bulletins also include monthly auction-by-mail sales. These lists are helpful for many reasons in that they give the collector some idea of the going prices and an opportunity to fill in series of postcards. One can buy by mail without having to leave the living-room. The clubs and their publications can also help put one in touch with collectors of similar cards, and trading by mail can be carried on. Collectors of new view cards can exchange cards of their locality with collectors from all over the world.

In 1903 a newspaper editor in Glasgow lamented, 'In 10 years, Europe will be buried beneath picture postcards'. This was, of course, a prediction that never quite came true. The good cards, those that were new when the prediction was made, are now scarce and the high postal rate for postcards has brought back letter writing. The telephone can more easily carry those messages that are urgent and, although good quality art cards are still being published in many parts of the world, they are of little interest to today's dedicated deltiologist.

Although the subject under discussion here is pre-World War I picture postcards, it should be mentioned that there are many collectors of modern view postcards which are made by the photochrome process from color transparencies. Many of them are superb examples of modern color photography. These cards are also traded around the world by mail and there is an organisation to aid these collectors. This is the International View Card Club, Canadian Printing and Stationery, Inc., Post Card Services Division, P.O. Box 2314, Halifax, Nova Scotia, Canada.

There are many advantages in collecting only chrome cards. The prices for them are rather stable the world over so that they can be traded fairly among collectors in various countries. One can own cards from almost any country in the world without going further than the local post office. There are some local chrome card collecting clubs. Collecting modern cards is an inexpensive hobby from which one can learn a lot about geography and many other subjects.

Once you become involved, you become exposed to the various categories in which you might prefer to collect, new sources of information, as well as material and new friendships with collectors from every walk of life. Whether you have a small collection or own many thousands of postcards in very specialised categories, you will be amazed at how much new information is being discovered and shared by deltiologists every day.

From time to time there are exhibits of picture postcards open to the public at various museums. Since postcards are easy to display, pack and ship, many of these exhibits are shown at more than one museum. There are, however, two superb collections that are available in the United States for study. These are the Jefferson R. Burdick Collection of Postcards at the Metropolitan Museum in New York City and the Werner Von Boltenstern's World Wide Postcard Collection at the library of Loyola University of Los Angeles, California. Each of these collections contains over one million exhibits. The Postcard Museum in Canaan, Connecticut, is the only museum in the world devoted entirely to picture postcards.

3
The History of Picture Postcards

The postcard has been with us for so long that we tend to take it for granted. However, its origins are interesting and the use of a card on which one could send a short message through the post at reduced rates was a cause for which several men fought. They finally won the battle, but not without the usual indifference that innovative ideas frequently receive. It was largely through the efforts of one man that the postal card finally became a reality slightly over one hundred years ago in Germany.

The postcard was introduced as an answer to a need to simplify correspondence. In order to write a letter in the nineteenth century a certain amount of preparation was required. Ink, pen and stationery all had to be collected into one place. More than that, custom dictated a certain form of salutation, body and closing. Sealing wax and seal must be nearby to close the envelope and even a simple message sent through the post could not, because of custom, be brief and to the point. One must first inquire after the health of the recipient and state one's own condition of health. One had to ask after various other members of the family and perhaps give a bit of local news. Because it was expensive to send a letter, paper was not wasted and inveterate letter writers learned to use every available inch of space. In some countries the postal charge was paid by the recipient rather than the sender which placed a further obligation upon the writer to make the letter worth the money.

The first creator of the idea of a postal card was Heinrich von Stephan, of the German Empire. His idea, put forth in 1865, was that a simple card should be printed on which a brief message could be written and which could be mailed without an envelope. At the same time Dr. Emmanuel Hermann of the Military Academy of Wiener-Neustadt had a similar idea. Both proposals were independent of one another and there is no evidence that either knew the other was going to enter his proposal at one of two sittings of the General Postal Conference held at Karlsruhe in 1865.

It was felt by both men that 'forms for open communications should be at the disposal of the public at the post offices and be obtainable of local and rural postmen'. The forms were to be of the dimensions of a good-sized envelope and would be called 'postal leaflets'. The front would have as the title the name of the postal district and a 'corresponding design' such as the coat-of-arms of the country. A space would be reserved on the left for

New groups of collectors have sprung up in the United States and Great Britain since World War II. This postcard marks the postcard centennial celebrated all over the world in 1969. It is made in the style of an old 'Gruss aus' and cards illustrated on it are of historical importance.

24

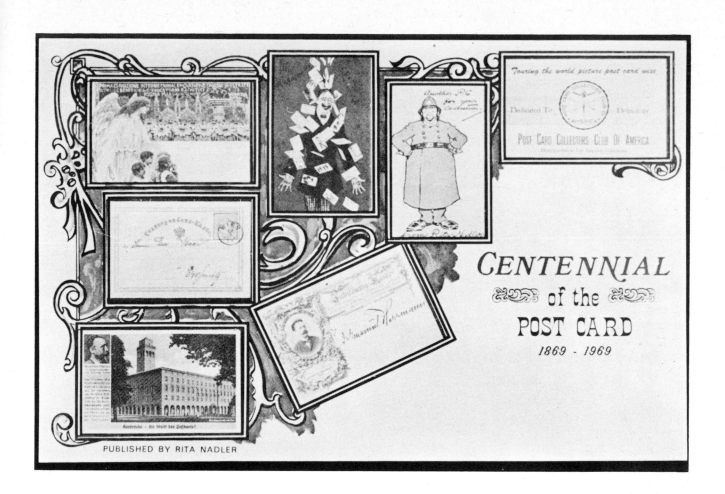

CENTENNIAL of the POST CARD 1869 - 1969

PUBLISHED BY RITA NADLER

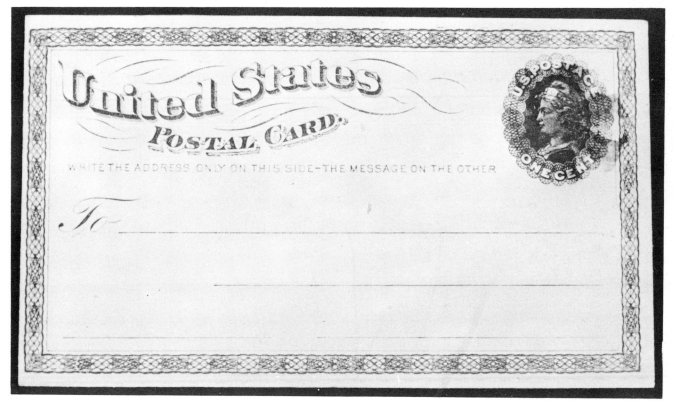

Earliest government (imprinted stamp) postal card issued by U.S. government.

the date stamp, the postage stamp would be printed in the right-hand corner and the space below would be reserved for the address and the notice, 'The back can be used for communications of all kinds which, as well as the address, may be written in ink, with ordinary or colored pencils, etc. If pencils are used care must be taken that all the inscriptions, especially the address, are distinct and indelible'. Mailable money orders had previously been

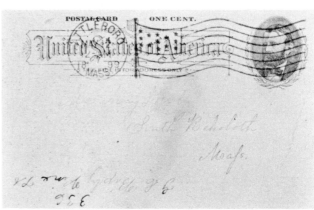

introduced by the German postal system and were made on a similar pattern.

Von Stephan's proposal was not accepted for discussion by the Director-General of Post. Professor Hermann's idea, published in a copy of the *Neue Freie Presse*, 26 January, 1869, under the title, 'A New Way of Corresponding Through the Post', stressed the lowering of cost of postage through the use of postcards and

Opposite.
1st row: US postal cards issued on September 30th, 1873 (left) and August 24th, 1885 (right).
2nd row: (left) US postal card issued on December 1st, 1886: (right) this card with Grant as imprinted stamp was first issued by US government on December 16th, 1891.
3rd row: (left) US postal card issued first on January 2nd, 1894; (right) US postal card cancelled in 1899.
4th row: McKinley postal cards cancelled in 1903.

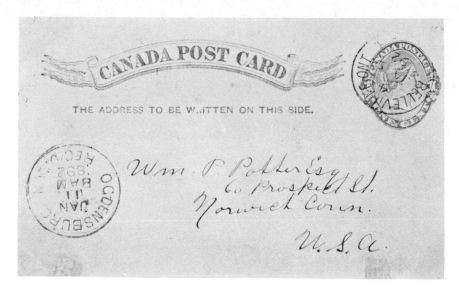

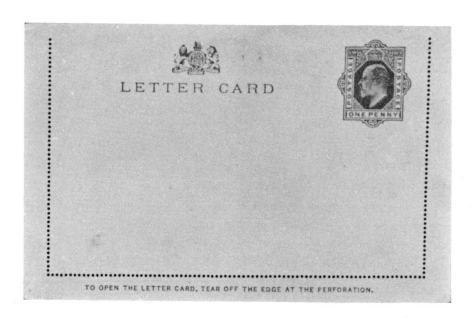

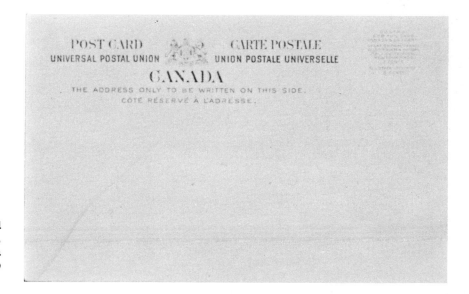

Top. Canadian governmental postal card cancelled in 1892. Center. British letter card with perforated sides and (bottom) bilingual Canadian postcard.

the advantages to the letter handlers. He said that the use of writing paper and envelopes, plus the elaborate writing style of the day, made letter writing an expensive occupation and recommended a twenty-word limit on postal cards, which he likened to a kind of 'postal telegram'.

27

The Director-General of the Austrian Post, intrigued with Professor Hermann's idea, issued the first government postal card, eschewing Hermann's suggestion of the name and calling it a 'Correspondence Card' instead. On October 1, 1869, the first government-issued correspondence card, of brownish tint, the thickness of a playing card, with the imperial eagle in the middle and a decorative border, was issued. The North German Con-

German 'Gruss aus' cards such as that at the top of this illustration usually had several pictorial views of the city or town for which it was made.

28

World's Columbian Exposition heralded beginning of souvenir views in United States.

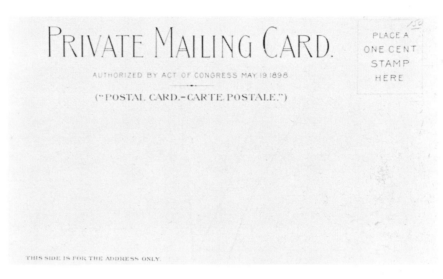

Act of Congress on May 19, 1898, authorized use of private mailing cards. Lower is a souvenir of the Pan-American Exposition in Buffalo, N.Y., in 1901.

federation followed shortly after with their own correspondence card. The postal card was immediately popular and brought extra revenue.

While the first postal cards were pre-stamped and paid for by the sender, the British Treasury did not look into the possibility of issuing postage stamps in that country until 1839. Previous to that time postage, as it was in many other countries, was paid for by the recipient on delivery. Since the charge was based on the number of sheets used plus the envelope, envelopes were seldom

PRINTED MATTER
SOUVENIR MAIL CARD
THIS SIDE FOR ADDRESS ONLY

Postage
One Cent
with no writing
on other side
—
Two Cents
otherwise

M

The U.S. government charged extra when more than just the address was written.

used at that time. The letters were simply folded and sealed with wax. Stationery with elaborate decorations printed on it later became popular. The first stamp issued in England was designed by William Mulready of the Royal Academy and it covered the entire surface of an envelope and elaborately conveyed, through symbolism, British postal benefits being conferred on the world. Decorated envelopes were soon published by a number of engravers and lithographers, many of them poking fun at the Mulready envelope.

The first British government postal card was issued in October, 1870. These were buff or violet colored and sold with an imprinted halfpenny stamp. Seventy-six million of these cards were sold the first year.

In the United States the Postmaster General recommended the issue of a government postal card in 1870, but Congress did not approve and a year-and-a-half later a similar bill was again introduced and passed with the President signing it into law on

World's Columbian Exposition 'Official Souvenir Postal' with view of the Woman's Building and portrait of Mrs Potter Palmer of Chicago.

OFFICIAL SOUVENIR POSTAL

MRS. POTTER PALMER.

WORLD'S COLUMBIAN EXPOSITION.

THE WOMAN'S BUILDING.

30

Anyone could publish postal cards as soon as the U.S. government gave up the monopoly and authorized private printing on which an adhesive stamp could be affixed. Publishers developed their own colophons and letter style.

8 June 1872. One should keep in mind that it had already been possible to send a piece of cardboard through the mail if it were properly addressed and a stamp affixed. However, here we are concerned with the cards that have been issued by various governments with imprinted stamps. These are called 'pioneer postcards' by deltiologists and are of interest as the forerunners of picture postcards. Stamp collectors and postal historians have a different interest in these government issued cards.

In 1870, the same year that the United States considered adopting government postal cards, France was under siege by the German army. The most expedient method of making contact with the rest of the world was to send up small balloons that would carry a limited amount of mail. Because weight was obviously a problem, small postcards were issued by private printers that were sold in stationers' shops and at tobacconists and their use was encouraged by the government. Obviously, these balloon flights were less than dependable and much of the cargo never reached its intended destination. It would be two more years before the French Government would formally adopt the official postal card.

The earliest recorded postcard in the world was one devised by John P. Charlton of Philadelphia, Pa., who obtained a copyright in

31

1861. The copyright was later transferred to H. Lipman of the same city. This was, of course, a private mailing card and had no part in the history of pre-stamped government cards. However, the idea was extremely innovative and obviously must have influenced later developments. The earliest known Lipman card used postally is dated 25 October 1870, and they were sold and used until 1873 when the government issued the pre-stamped postal cards.

The Lipman card was a plain message example, bearing the inscription, 'Lipman's Postal Card' in the upper left hand corner. In addition a 'patent applied for' paragraph was printed below. The second issue of this card included a squared-off space for the stamp on the right and is better known among pioneer deltiologists since there are only a few known specimens of the earlier issue.

Government-issued postal cards enjoyed a rather long monopoly until the advent of the privately printed picture postcard, which became popular at different times in different countries and for different reasons. As will be pointed out later in more detail (see chapter on fairs and expositions) the World Columbian Exhibition of 1893, held in Chicago, popularised view cards in the United States which were issued at that event for the first time. An act of Congress on 19 May 1898 gave the right to private publishers to publish cards that could be mailed for

32

There is No Distance Love Cannot Span

Love Knows No Limit, Since Earth Began.

To my Valentine

"find when love speaks, the voice of all the gods
Makes heaven drowsy with the harmony."
Shakespeare

2049—4

To my Valentine

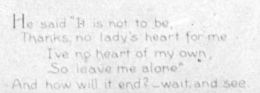

He said "It is not to be,
Thanks, no lady's heart for me
I've no heart of my own,
So leave me alone"
And how will it end?—wait, and see.

A HAPPY NEW YEAR

Along the lane
you tread to-day,
And thro' the
coming year,
May smiling sunbeams
round you play,
And fragrant
blossoms cheer.

With Love and Devotion

"Bought a ring for fourty shillin,
Which thou mayest wear if thou art willin."

Christmas Greetings

When you gather
around the Christmas tree.
And admire the gifts prepared for thee.
When you enjoy all Christmas Cheer
Think of me and my wishes sineere

Top: a Clapsaddle composition with children in eighteenth-century costume. Bottom: outdoor group on Christmas card by Ellen Clapsaddle shows her feeling for composition.

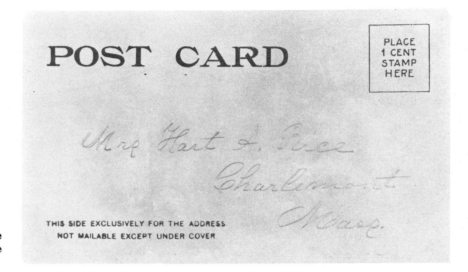

Early photographic example with photograph on message side.

the same rate as the government cards, and these were to be inscribed, 'Private Mailing Card – Authorised by Act of Congress, May 19, 1898'. This act put many postcard manufacturers into business and the collecting of their products as a hobby became almost immediately popular in the United States.

American collectors were somewhat behind their British counterparts in amassing as many picture postcards as possible. Shortly following the printing of government postals in Austria and Germany, picture postcards were produced privately in those countries. The postal rate used at first was not reduced, but the German Government, upon seeing the immediate popularity of these cards lowered the postal rate to that of its own.

The Paris Exhibition of 1882 popularised the picture postcard in France and the Royal Naval Exhibition in London in 1891 was advertised on postcards that were sold on the top of the Eddystone Lighthouse replica that was built for that event. As with the French postcards that were sold at the top of the new Eiffel Tower in 1882, these could be purchased, written on and mailed at the top of the tower.

By 1890 the assurance of the popularity of picture postcards brought about the publication of many view and greeting cards and collectors began to buy every item they could find that appealed to them and would look good in their albums. For the next quarter-century deltiology became a widespread hobby that

35

was extremely lucrative for artists, photographers, printers and publishers.

Some of the earliest picture postcards that were to influence strongly their subsequent designs and purposes, were the cards printed in Austria and Germany with multiple scenes of a city and the message 'Gruss aus –' with the name of the town or city from which the postcard was sent. The traveler could then fill the space left under the pictures for the address and write a message on the reverse side to friends and relatives back home. Since room had to be left on the front for the address, the pictures were, of necessity, quite small. In the earliest history of the picture postcard the pictures were always limited to allow room for the address and stamp.

The first country to sanction divided back postcards, on which one side was used for the address, message and the stamp and the entire opposite side of the card could be reserved for a picture, was France. On 18 November 1903, the French Minister of Commerce, Industry, Posts and Telegraph authorised the use of illustrated cards on which the address side was divided into two sections, the left side for a message and the right for the address and stamp. The Universal Postal Union authorised the use of divided address cards shortly afterwards.

Most collectors recognise all undivided back cards as having been made prior to 1903, but a great many were made following the authorisation of the divided backs. Some cards are still being printed in this manner, depending upon the artistic design placed on them. Those that have dated cancellations are, of course, the easiest to place in the history of the picture postcard.

There are other elements besides the picture to be considered as part of the interest. The graphic artist will find an almost unlimited amount of letter styles in the word 'postcard' that is printed on many of the early cards. Ingenious artistic methods of drawing a centre line on the backs of the divided cards and publisher's colophons can be found in both the *art nouveau* and *art deco* printing styles. However, the majority of the lettering is done in fancier Victorian style. Interesting cancellations and stamps are a bonus to the postcard collector who would prefer to find examples that are pristine and unused. Picture postcards were used and mailed all over the world and stamp collectors are interested in them from their own point of view.

There are, perhaps, no better examples of the lithographer's art than on the picture postcards made between the time of their popularisation and the beginning of World War I. Lithography, the process of printing from stone, was invented by a German, Aloys Senefelder, in 1796. His early work was done in black and white, but he later invented a color process. Many nineteenth-century artists used lithography as a medium for reproducing works of art. The manufacturers used lithography as a means of producing huge quantities of brightly colored cards. The immediate popularity of postcards with pictures on them in color made it possible for them to be sold at low prices. Although the process of lithography was fairly expensive, a single popular card might be produced by the hundreds of thousands once the stones were prepared. Dies were also made for the embossing that we find on many of the old German postcards. Since the lithographic process is costly (a stone had to be prepared for each color placed on the card), like cards are not made today. The techniques by which picture postcards of pre-World War I vintage were produced will

36

Authorized by Act of Congress of May 19 1898

Title from address side of a private mail card, showing government authorization.

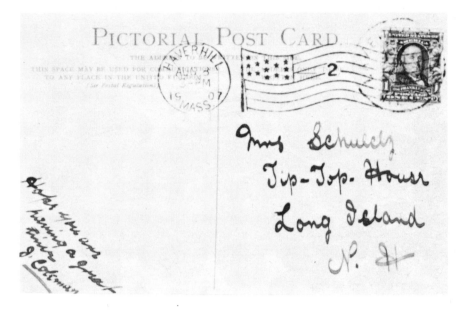

PICTORIAL POST CARD

By 1907 divided backs were in general use. 'Pictorial Post Card' is unusual title.

never be revived. Those who collect these beautifully designed, embossed, tiny lithographs are truly amassing a miniature gallery of examples of the lithographer's art at its best.

Those collectors of early photographic postcards are also aware that their cards are representative of a type of photography that was innovative and difficult for the time. The wet plate process of photography was not invented until 1851 and had been used with success by Mathew Brady in photographing the Civil War. This process necessitated spreading a solution on glass plates and exposing the plate while still wet and developing it immediately. Brady and William H. Jackson, who photographed the early American Western explorations had to have wagons equipped with darkrooms so that they could develop their plates immediately after the photograph had been taken.

George Eastman simplified the photographic process by inventing roll film in the 1880s. This could be used in hand-held cameras. Most of the early photographs for postcards, however, were taken with heavy view cameras that were loaded onto wagons by the traveling photographers that were hired by German postcard publishers and printers. Photographic equipment that we take for granted today was not commercially available until rather late. Flash bulbs, for instance, were not introduced until 1929 and color film, originated by Eastman Kodak, was introduced commercially in 1935. The invention of Kodachrome film made possible the inexpensive, brightly colored photographic postcards that we have today.

4
Publishers

The story of picture postcards in terms of the people who published them is a confusing one. It might do well for the new collector to keep in mind that most frequently the publisher was not the printer. Most of the cards sold before World War I were printed in Germany or Austria. Printers in this area of Europe were expert in the art of lithography and seemed to have an excellent understanding of the many methods that could be used to create artistic cards from the small oblongs of cardboard.

Raphael Tuck, the largest British publisher of picture postcards, used printers in Germany to produce many of their cards. Records of many of the important postcard publishers have been lost or destroyed through two wars and our only evidence as to who published what cards is often the information we can find on the cards themselves. Frequently, the publishers used no mark of identification and often used only a monogram or letter since the space available for identifying themselves on either side was somewhat limited. Laws regarding the registration of business names in England postdate the manufacture of most of the collectible cards and it was not until 22 December 1916, that business names had to be registered in that country.

The identification of American postcard publishers is also confusing and searches are extremely unrewarding. Anyone, from the owner of the corner drugstore to a lady looking to supplement her income, could be a postcard publisher. One had only to submit photographs or art work to the many agents kept in countries all over the world by the German printers who in turn saw that the postcards were printed and delivered. Frequently, an artist's picture was copyrighted and this mark sometimes will identify for the collector the publisher who held the copyright. Less frequently, the artist owned the rights to the design. It was not unusual for people already in some area of the publishing business such as newspapers or other periodicals to become postcard publishers and/or distributors.

Perhaps the best known publisher is the aforementioned Tuck company. There are many collectors who specialise only in Tuck cards and even these specialists could never hope to own all examples of the hundreds of thousands published by that firm. Tuck were already established 'art publishers to the Queen' by the time they entered the postcard publishing business and their reputation as producers of fine quality prints was well established. Their greeting cards were popular before the postcard boom and Tuck's reputation for quality printing continued to be well-earned. There are so many series of subjects used by Tuck that it would be impossible to list them all in one book. Tuck purchased the art work of many of the leading illustrators of the period and collectors look for cards by Harry Payne, Asti, Louis Wain, Professor von Hier, Phil May and many others.

1st row: headings were graphically beautiful; (left) American eagle and draped flag, with (right) art nouveau design showing Cupid carrying letter. 2nd, 3rd, 4th rows: address side of undivided back postcards illustrating graphic art work of the period. The left-hand card in the 3rd row is from Indo-China.
5th row: (left) Canadian souvenir with beaver design in corner; (right) elaborate divided back Canadian souvenir.

38

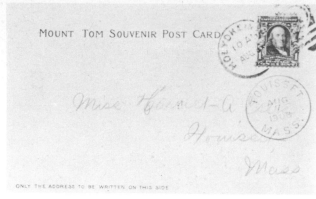

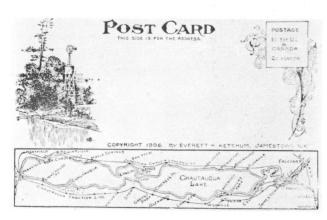

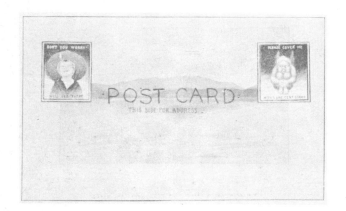

The subjects treated by Tuck's artists are numerous and varied. There were, for instance, at least six hundred series (usually of six cards each) of ocean views. Many of the cards made for export to foreign markets by Tuck have never been seen in England. For instance, Harry Payne's series of 'Wild West of America' would not have been of interest to British collectors unless they specialised in the work of Harry Payne. Royalty of England as well as heads of state of other countries were subjects of many Tuck cards. Tuck's postcards were printed in numbered, titled series to appeal to the avid collectors of the first fifteen years of this century. Limited edition proof sets were published and advertised by Tuck for collectors who wanted the better than ordinary artist-designed cards for their albums.

There were, of course, many other outstanding British publishers of picture postcards, some of whom are still in business. One of these is Bamforth & Co., Holmfirth, Yorkshire, whose illustrated song cards are very much in demand by deltiologists. Millar and Lang produced many kinds of collectible items among

Many address sides became so crowded with lettering and illustration that there was sometimes little room left.

40

which are some 'Hands across the sea' cards that are popular among collectors.

Another large British publisher whose cards were once desirable collectors' items and have become so once again is the Inter-Art Co. Its cards were all numbered and in series and the firm bought the work of good illustrators such as Lawson Wood, Donald McGill and A. A. Nash.

Another greeting card publisher who became known for his high quality picture postcards is Valentine & Sons, Dundee. Valentine was best known for the publication of superb view cards and a collector of these would have an almost complete idea of what the British Isles looked like at the turn of the century. Valentine also made many novelty items such as die-cut pull-outs and jewelled pictures.

Wrench of London was another important publisher of view cards. Wrench was the earliest publisher to realise the wealth of subjects for picture postcards in the world's museums and they reproduced pictures of sculpture and paintings to be sold at museums and elsewhere. Wrench also made photographic cards

Patriotic symbols, drawings and photographs were commonly used to decorate address sides.

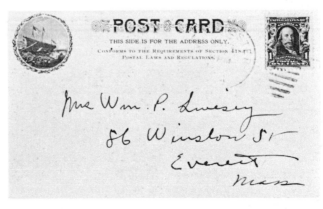

41

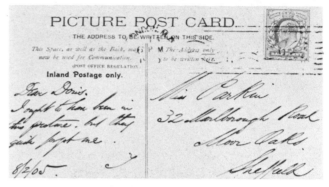

42

NEW LONDON, NEW HAMPSHIRE

POST CARD

AUTHORIZED BY ACT OF CONGRESS MAY 19, 1898.

PLACE POSTAGE STAMP HERE

Post Card.

GEM VIEW CO.

Sprange Souvenir Series

BEACH BLUFF, MASS.

Place a One Cent Stamp here

Souvenir of PORTLAND, ME

POST CARD

This side for the address.

Published by C.H. BROWN MIDDLE ST

Place Postage Stamp Here

Opposite.
1st, 2nd rows: divided backs – 3 spellings show international use. Top right card was printed in Canada. Right-hand cards (1st, 2nd rows) have backs explaining purpose. 3rd row: (left) heavy embossing made writing difficult; (right) attractive lettering interspersed with 4-leaf clovers. 4th, 5th rows: these 4 show lettering variety. Bottom right card is Greek.
Above.
Top: towns and cities had cards printed as a form of advertisement, as these headings show. Center: before the turn of the century, souvenirs were published in series for albums. Bottom: a souvenir of Portland, Maine.

of animals and many political cards that were made from cartoons that had appeared in *Punch* and other periodicals.

Many publishers were known for their publication of the work of outstanding artists. The International Art Co. of America was Ellen H. Clapsaddle's major publisher although this prolific artist also did work for several other publishers in America, England and Germany. The Ullman Mfg. Co. of New York was the first publisher of Bertha L. Corbett's 'Sunbonnet Babies'.

Some of the more prolific publishers of American view cards were the American News, New York; A. C. Bosselman & Co., New York; V. O. Hammon, Chicago and Minneapolis; E. C. Kropp, Milwaukee; Metropolitan News Co., Boston; Detroit Publishing Co., Detroit; Illustrated Postal Card Co., New York; H. C. Leighton Co., Portland, Maine; Edward H. Mitchell, San Francisco; The Souvenir Postcard Co., New York; and Curt Teich & Co., Chicago. In 1910 the Hugh C. Leighton Co. combined its business with Valentine & Sons Publishing Co. of New York and London.

If many of the above names of American postcard publishers appear to have Germanic roots it is, of course, not mere coincidence. As the business began to flourish many of the German printers opened agencies in the United States. British publishing firms, including Tuck, also kept offices in the United States.

The design and manufacture of picture postcards was an international business and although the product sold for pennies, the amounts purchased were so enormous that the business became extremely profitable. There were many large international firms and many more small local publishers. There are some publishers who might have produced only a few issues and who are known for just one particular picture postcard. In cases where an advertising card for a firm was manufactured by a printer to order for the firm, the firm became the publisher. This is true of the ship postcards that were distributed free to passengers. In this case, the shipping firm was the publisher.

The one attempt to list and identify postcard publishers' trademarks is a privately printed book called *Publishers' Trademarks Identified* written by the late Walter E. Corson and edited by James L. Lowe (see Bibliography). Over fifteen hundred trademarks are listed and illustrated in this rather ambitious work which includes some modern publishers as well as those who flourished when the picture postcard craze was in its heyday. Publishers can often, but not always, be identified by many of the marks appearing here. One of the problems is that designs were copied by small companies and when the card was copied, so were all identifying marks. In addition, such a list can never be truly complete. There were too many small publishers who used no identifying marks on their cards, others who copied another publisher's letter style in the word 'Postcard', which is a means of identifying some publishers, and thousands upon thousands of other cards for which the printer was the 'publisher' and many of these cards have only 'made in Germany' printed on the message side.

Collectors tend to specialise in the marked cards of companies such as Tuck or Detroit and these are the publishers whose issues will eventually increase in value beyond the unidentifiable ones. Collecting cards by publisher is a safe investment for any deltiologist. As more research is done and published by collectors, many more of the outstanding postcards will be listed and identified as to who the publishers were. Meanwhile, it would be sad to see the entire hobby of deltiology bound by so much esoteric information that we can no longer accept and keep a card that we like simply because it is appealing artistically.

Backs of postcards became almost as decorative as other side. Some were issued on board ship to be sent home by travellers.

44

5

Signed Artists' Cards

It should be obvious by now that many of the picture postcards that come under specialty headings were signed by the artists who designed them. That is, the original painting, etching or drawing was signed. When these postcard artists have an easily recognisable style that made their work popular when it was originally done and their signatures are clearly visible, the postcards that they designed are eagerly sought by today's collectors. Signed cards, particularly those of certain artists who worked in the area of book illustration and postcard design at the beginning of this century or were otherwise well known in the field of commercial or fine art, are the cream of any deltiologist's collection and the field is one in which the most serious research has been done. However, the field is so vast that there is certainly room for more research and information concerning the favourite artist-designed cards. The situation is further complicated by the fact that many obviously capable artists will always remain anonymous or will be known only by their initials.

Many of the artists who worked for postcard publishers signed only their initials or used a pseudonym rather than have their professional names known among their fellow artists. For many, the postcard work was only a means of making enough money to support the painter in his pursuit of the finer arts. It is interesting that a great many of those artists who attempted to remain anonymous in the area of postcard design by using pseudonyms, initials or no signature at all might have faded into oblivion were it not for the pictures they made for the postcard publishers. The craze for the enormous variety and amount of postcards at the beginning of this century made it possible for many artists who might otherwise have starved to make a rather decent living helping to supply this demand for an almost unlimited number of designs.

The media of a small decorated cardboard surface led to the design of some rather superior folk art and in order to understand the variation in art styles to be found on picture postcards one must know something about the changes that took place in the world of fine and applied art toward the end of the last century. A few of the better known artists who were innovative and important in other areas of art were also involved to some extent in the design of picture postcards. The Czech artist, Alphonse Mucha, was one of the men who had found success in the 'new art' of the period. Mucha worked in Paris and designed posters for Sarah Bernhardt.

The development of poster art preceded the turn of the century and the bright lithographed posters that were displayed in the

Postcard in art nouveau style signed by Mucha.

45

By the Light of the Lanterns.

A Sunny Temple.

Bearing a Baksan.

Umbrellas and Commerce.

Daughters of the Sun.

major cities of Europe had a strong influence on the artist-designed postcards. However, poster art and postcard art were developed to appeal to the public on different levels. The poster was an advertising device, made to catch the eye and convey a message to the viewer at a single glance. Postcards could be of this type also, but could require somewhat longer study if the viewer wished. Although they were cheap and were meant originally to convey a short message through the mail, as soon as the hobby of collecting them grew to such enormous proportions, the postcards were collected and inserted in albums in pristine condition.

Although relatively few picture postcards were designed in the *art nouveau* style, the languorous, ephemeral style of drawing that appealed to the young innovative artists in England, Belgium, France and Germany, there are many that show the influence of *art nouveau*. The innovations, particularly in the area of lithography, were important to the postcard designers who had to understand that medium of printing on paper through the use of inked stones. The flat planes and simplicity of line in the cards of Paul Ebner show some of the influences brought about by the *art nouveau* movement. The dark outlines and economy of detail in the cards designed by Ethel Parkinson are also direct results of the arts and crafts movement and ultimately the new art. Many cards have borders or vignettes of the simplified languid

Scenes of Japan painted by Mortimer Menpes. He was especially adept at painting children.

Opposite.
Artist E. P. Kinsella devised this appealing urchin at play in the 1st and 2nd rows.
3rd row: Jenny Nystrom designed and signed these appealing Christmas cards.

46

"HOW'S THAT?"

QUT FOR HIS COUNTY

"THE CATCH OF THE SEASON."

"THE BOSS."

Merry Christmas

Glad påsk!

God Jul

plants and stems that were typical of the *art nouveau* style. However, *art nouveau* was a popular style among only a few commercial artists and the best of the postcards designed in this manner are the 'Twelve Months' series by Alphonse Mucha.

Many of the artists who designed picture postcards derived a part of their income from the illustration of children's books. Frances Brundage, an American, worked for Raphael Tuck in both capacities. She illustrated *A Peep At The World's Fair*, a children's book of the World's Industrial Fair in New Orleans in 1885. Other Brundage designs were taken from earlier illustrations for children's books. Kate Greenaway, the well-known illustrator of children's books, designed some postcards for Marcus Ward, publishers. Miss Greenaway died in 1902 but her designs were continually popular and many of her postcards, although quite rare today, were published after her death. The Greenaway illustrations were used mainly for Christmas and Valentine greeting cards and such is Kate Greenaway's continual popularity in the United States that her books are currently being reprinted and there is a Kate Greenaway Society

Greeting cards designed and signed by Mailick. Many of them are highlighted in gold.

48

The Village Smithy.

The Village pump.

Turning the thrashing machine

Winter in the Lane.

The Farm in Winter.

The prolific artist Harry Payne painted hundreds of scenes for Tuck.

formed for the study and collection of her many illustrations. Miss Greenaway's paintings of children dressed in nineteenth-century costume have periodically influenced children's clothing styles in this century. Although postcards with Greenaway designs that can be found today were made for the most part after Miss Greenaway's death, they are still highly thought of by many collectors.

Florence Hardy was another artist who used children as her subjects. She painted them in Dutch costume and also used eighteenth-century ladies and their suitors as postcard subjects. Her cards were designed for Faulkner.

A most prolific artist who was also a book illustrator was Harry Payne. He was well known for his illustrations for books on military history and his paintings for Tuck of a variety of uniformed soldiers are popular among collectors of Tuck or artist-signed cards. Payne's series on the 'Wild West of America' are somewhat less well known but are, of course, very desirable to American collectors. Payne painted men and horses with a vigorous realism.

Mortimer Menpes was a rather well-known artist, illustrator and writer who, as a young man, was a follower and student of James McNeill Whistler. He fell out of favor with Whistler when he left London to go to Japan to study Japanese art. Menpes was a talented artist capable of capturing the charm of children in his paintings and his own four children were

49

Hallowe'en

immortalised in an etching (no larger than postcard size) by Whistler that was later used for a frontispiece for a book, *Whistler As I Knew Him*, written by Menpes. The postcards designed by Menpes are part of the story of the art world in London at the turn of the century. Although Menpes never reached the stature as an artist that his 'Master' enjoyed, through the medium of picture postcards his paintings were well known to collectors and are sought still.

Menpes' sensitive illustrations of Japanese children are quite lovely and show a remarkable talent that, were it not for his necessary pursuit of money to support his large family, might have manifested itself in a greater and more lasting reputation in the fine arts.

By the end of the nineteenth century, art and illustration were considered acceptable occupations for women and many of them found their way into the lucrative field of postcard design. One American artist, Ellen H. Clapsaddle, stands out both for her

50

Beautifully lithographed post-cards from paintings by Asti.

remarkable talent and her prolificacy. Miss Clapsaddle was born in South Columbia, New York, in 1865, and she began drawing and painting at a very early age. As a young woman she painted designs for calendars and greeting cards, painted portraits and landscapes and hand-painted on china. It was only natural that at the beginning of the postcard craze in America, in 1905, Miss Clapsaddle should have turned her attention to postcard design since she had already formed an affiliation with the International Art Company for whom she painted designs for calendars and greeting cards.

Ellen Clapsaddle's pictures of children are especially sought by collectors today. She simplified the later documentation of her cards by signing many of them and painting in a style that is easily recognisable. Her children are ingenuous and charming and many of her painted subjects are often carefully integrated with the message or verse on her cards since she also wrote many of these. The children are round-faced and always dressed in charming costumes. Miss Clapsaddle also painted landscape scenes, animals and a series of cross-stitch sampler-type cards that are bright and colorful. Her style of art evidently could be easily adjusted to meet any demands placed upon her in the designing of several thousand greeting cards that she signed and she was as able in painting sophisticated adult cards as she was in devising her many designs that used children as subjects. She designed a series of 'Illuminated pages' greeting cards that show a remarkable talent in the field of lettering and graphic arts.

Ellen Clapsaddle rode high on the wave of success during the picture postcard craze and it is thought that artists were hired to color or finish the hundreds of paintings and sketches she designed. Miss Clapsaddle worked for several publishers at one time and became so involved in the design and manufacture of picture postcards that she invested her life savings in the International Art Publishing Company owned by the Wolf family with whom she had gotten her start. She was in Germany when World War I broke out and was brought out of Germany by friends, a penurious and sick woman. She died in New York in 1934.

Although the bulk of her work was published by the International Art Company (later to be called Wolf Advertising Company) this American publisher before World War I had its greeting cards, calendars and postcards printed in Germany. Miss Clapsaddle also did work for other publishers, among whom were Raphael Tuck and Sons.

Another American woman artist who designed cards for Tuck was Frances Brundage. She was the daughter of Rembrandt Lockwood, a painter of church murals from Newark, New Jersey. Frances illustrated Louisa May Alcott's books as well as other juvenile books and had established a national reputation as an illustrator. She was hired by the New York office of the Tuck Company sometime around the end of the century to do some illustrations for their juvenile book list and was therefore well established as a company artist shortly before the postcard craze. Many of the early Brundage card designs were illustrations taken from her books. Frances Brundage-signed postcards have either the artist's full signature or her initials in oriental style superimposed one on the other.

There were many other artists who specialised in children as subjects for their postcard designs. Most of the illustrators of

53

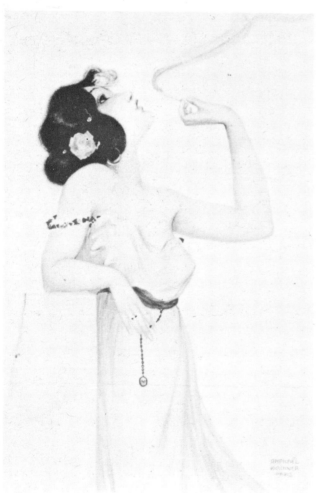

Raphael Kirchner was the creator of the modern pin-up girl. These four are from famous 'cigarettes du monde' series. Model is his wife, Nina. These French cards were extremely daring for the time.

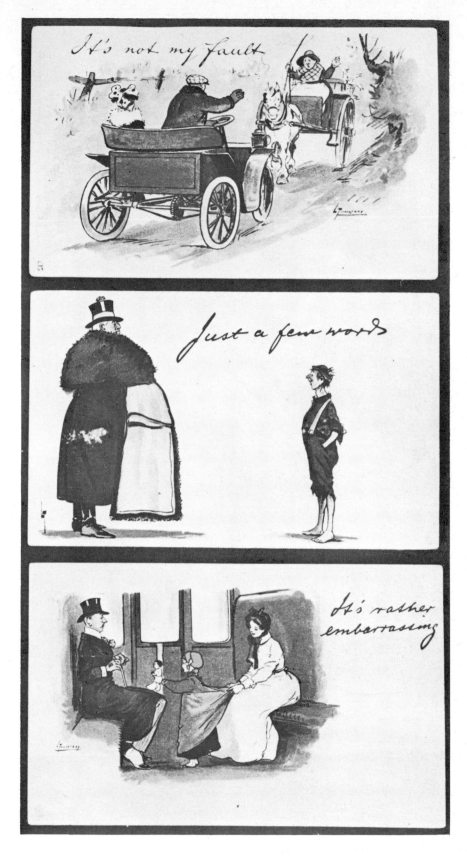

It's not my fault

Just a few words

It's rather embarrasing

Artist Lance Thackeray designed many such 'Amewsing Write-Away' cards for Tuck.

children were, not surprisingly, women. Katherine Gassaway drew wide-eyed cartoon-type children. The American, Rose O'Neill, invented the cherubic 'Kewpie' with the pointed head. The O'Neill kewpie had wide appeal as dolls and carnival give-aways when they were first designed and is once again enjoying immense popularity among American collectors. The 'Sunbonnet babies' were first designed by an American woman artist, Bertha L. Corbett. These cards were so popular that they were later adapted by other postcard artists, especially Dr. Bernhardt

Drink to-day and drown all sorrow;
Maybe you'll be gone to-morrow;
While you have it, use your breath;
There's no drinking after death.

May bad luck follow you all your days
and never overtake you.

There's always a song to the future,
To the years that stretch on ahead,
There's always a toast to the things that are new,
To life's books which have never been read.

But here's to what lies behind us,
To the heartaches, the failures, the tears,
We are better able for just those things
To drink to the future years.

God made man
Frail as a bubble;
God made Love,
Love made Trouble;
God made the Vine—
Was it a sin
That man made Wine
To drown Trouble in?

56

These 'framed' dark background postcards were designed by Dwig, also for Tuck.

Wall. There are about seventy or more designs including sunbonnet babies and there are at least a dozen series or groups. Artist E. P. Kinsella invented an adorable urchin with a too-big hat and one suspender and used him on postcards.

Contemporary artists and illustrators who were somewhat more serious in their motifs are represented in the signed artist picture postcards. M. Billings was famous for his studies in still life of flowers and fruit. These were published by Tuck. Another artist, contemporary with the postcard boom, was Professor von Hier. His paintings show a remarkable resemblance to other pre-impressionists working in England at the time and exhibit an unusual talent if not much originality of style. M. Wielandt's views of France are superb contemporary studies of the French countryside. Another artist well known to today's picture post-card collectors is Kyd who painted characters from Dickens' novels. Kyd designed several of these series for Raphael Tuck.

Raphael Kirchner was famous for his *art nouveau* cards, the subjects of which were languid girls or girls in rather sexy poses. Kirchner's 'Cigarettes du Monde' series in which he used his wife as a model was extremely popular and all too prophetic. Kirchner's wife-model became addicted, not to cigarettes, but to narcotics, and spent her last years in a mental institution.

The designers of many comic postcards are also well known to advanced collectors. Some of the better known artists of this type of card are Arthur Gill, known for his drawings of cats; Donald McGill, who designed over three thousand comic postcards that were immensely popular at the time of their publication; Phil May, a *Punch* cartoonist who designed many of the Tuck 'Write-Away' series; Tom Browne, who signed many of his cards 'Tom B.'; and many others.

As one can readily see, the list of artists who signed their cards will probably never be complete for new ones are constantly turning up. Collectors tend to look for those artist-signed cards that have special appeal for them, whether it is the sophisticated art style of Billings or the comic cards of Browne or May. The compilation of a list of the work of some of the more prolific artists such as Ellen H. Clapsaddle or Donald McGill can become the work of a single dedicated deltiologist that will occupy many months of his time. When these check-lists are finally published they are, perhaps, the most helpful information other postcard collectors can find.

One artist, Charles Baldwyn, worked for the Worcester porcelain company as a plate decorator. His specialty was bird paintings and he supplemented his income by designing picture postcards. Mabel Lucie Atwell was known for her paintings of chubby children; L. Barribel painted sultry red-headed women for the Inter-Art Publishing Company; F. Earl Christy, Howard Chandler Christy, E. C. Curtis, Eva Danniell, Paul de Longpré, H. B. Griggs, Mary Golay, G. Gretty, Jenny Harbour, Helen Jackson and John A. Heyermans are all names that might have faded into the oblivion of the art world were it not that they designed pictures for the many card publishers in existence at the beginning of this century. While some of them made names for themselves in other areas of art, it is probable that the popularity of the picture postcard kept most of them in pencils, brushes and paint.

57

6

Fairs and Expositions

During a period when communication was not as rapid as it is today, fairs and expositions were more apt to affect the standards of popular taste. The large expositions grew out of the commercial fairs of Asia and Europe and the first exposition of international scope was the Great Exposition sponsored by Prince Albert in London in 1851. The Crystal Palace, erected in Hyde Park, was the prototype for a smaller but similar building erected in New

Two postcards from 1900 Exposition in Paris.

58

Photographic cards from 1900 Exposition Universelle show Eiffel tower and fantastic buildings constructed around its base and along banks of Seine.

York for a less successful exposition venture several years later.

Large expositions were also held in Paris in 1867, 1889 and 1900. The 1889 exposition of Paris is of particular interest to collectors since it heralded the birth in France of the picture postcard as a souvenir of such an event. The Eiffel Tower was built for the 1889 Exposition and cards were sold that could be addressed and mailed from the top of the remarkable building. The message most frequently written on such cards was, not surprisingly, 'I am writing this card from the top of this tower'.

The Eiffel Tower figured prominently again in the Paris Exposition of 1900 when a group of fantastic other-world buildings were erected around its base and along the banks of the Seine. By 1900 the rage for picture postcards was well-entrenched among travelers and stay-at-homes alike and a wide variety of postcards celebrating this great fair were printed.

In America no postcards were made in 1876 to remind one of the great centennial celebration in Philadelphia. Advertising and album cards were made as souvenirs and although many of these

59

Postcards from all fairs and expositions have been popular collectors' items during this century.

Left: first official pictorial postcards in the United States were made for the World's Columbian Exposition held in Chicago.

Right: advertising the Hudson-Fulton Celebration in 1909. Note dirigible with date as part of design.

60

Hudson Fulton

1809 - 1909

Celebration

Front of Trans-Mississippi and International Exposition card engraved and printed by the Chicago Colortype Co, and copyrighted in 1898 by the U.S. Postal Card Co.

Card from World's Fair, St Louis, Missouri, in 1904.

Postcard from Trans-Mississippi International Exposition showing view of the Machinery and Electricity Building.

are the approximate size of postcards they were not meant to be mailed unless tucked into an envelope.

The World's Columbian Exposition was the first American fair to make use of the picture postal card as a souvenir. The Exposition opened on 1 May 1893, and since the opening occurred a year after the original scheduled date there had been plenty of time for engravings to have been made of the various buildings and symbols of the fair to be used on postcards.

Charles W. Goldsmith was awarded a franchise for the Colum-

62

The Agricultural Palace at the Lewis and Clark Exposition in Portland, Oregon, in 1905. Note vignette with balloon and clock.

Postcard advertising the Alaska-Yukon Exposition held in Seattle, Washington in 1909. Art style is adapted from art nouveau style of European artists.

Postal card promoting the San Francisco Festival in 1910.

bian 'official card', a variety of views was chosen and vending machines that dispensed two cards for five cents were placed strategically around the grounds. Cards of this type were sold in Chicago before the fair opened and they were well received. Sets were then manufactured by fair officials and offered to the public at ten for twenty-five cents. The original early cards did not have the official seal of the fair or signatures of officials and these are known among deltiologists as 'pre-official'. There were several variations of the cards that were sold in sets and the views to be found on them are of the various buildings such as 'Government Building', 'Administrations Building', 'The Electrical Building',

63

Far left, left, and right: the opening of the Panama Canal was the reason for an exposition in San Francisco in 1915.

etc. A set of these in their original wrapper would be a particularly interesting find for any collectors interested in these early 'pioneer' postcards.

Besides the official cards there were other issues from the World's Columbian Exposition. Some were line drawings and others were photographic cards. Some were printed in black while others were printed in full color. A multi-view example has a composite illustration of an air view of the fair (a distinct innovation for the time) and is in the approximate form of a 'gruss aus' card. In addition to these unofficial cards there were several issues of advertising cards for the 1893 Chicago Fair.

The World's Columbian Exposition heralded a series of fairs and expositions in America and many cities followed with celebrations of their own. The Pan-American Exposition in Buffalo, New York, in 1901; the Louisiana Purchase Exposition in St. Louis, Missouri, in 1904; the Louis and Clark Exposition in Portland, Oregon, in 1905; the Tercentennial Exposition in Jamestown, Virginia, in 1907; the Alaska–Yukon–Pacific in Seattle, Washington, in 1909; the Panama–Pacific International Exposition in San Francisco in 1915 were the principal fairs held in the United States before that country entered the war in Europe. Postcards can be found for all of these fairs by determined collectors.

Previous to World War I there were so many fairs and expositions in America, England and the Continent that the selection of postcards made to commemorate them are still numerous. Many of the European cards were designed by the artists who also designed the posters advertising the fairs and the art work is contemporary with the period and of a rather good quality.

For collectors of novelty cards, the Paris Exposition of 1900 is noted for the issues of hold-to-light and other interesting novelty cards including some with inset transparencies. Some of the hold-to-lights made for this occasion are amusing in that the scenes are artificially darkened daylight scenes with full moons or stars in the sky.

The Paris 1900 Exposition was an occasion that truly popularised the picture postcard in France and throughout the world. The great variety of novelty cards and the photographic views of the rather fantastic buildings that were erected especially for the

From the 300th anniversary celebration of Jamestown, Virginia, in 1907. Curiously drawn maps were typical of art style at beginning of the century.

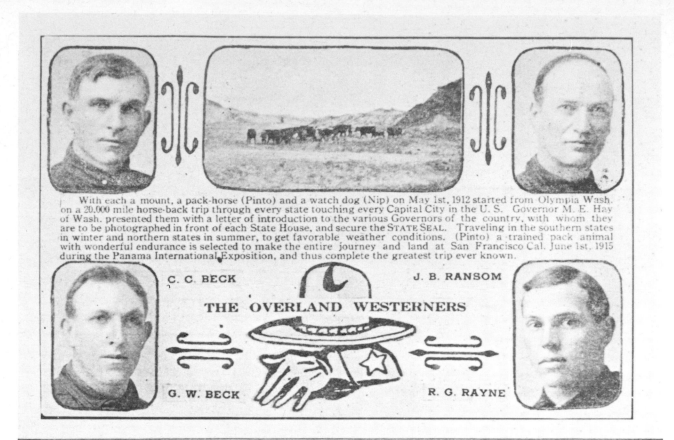

With each a mount, a pack-horse (Pinto) and a watch dog (Nip) on May 1st, 1912 started from Olympia Wash. on a 20,000 mile horse-back trip through every state touching every Capital City in the U. S. Governor M. E. Hay of Wash. presented them with a letter of introduction to the various Governors of the country, with whom they are to be photographed in front of each State House, and secure the STATE SEAL. Traveling in the southern states in winter and northern states in summer, to get favorable weather conditions. (Pinto) a trained pack animal with wonderful endurance is selected to make the entire journey and land at San Francisco Cal. June 1st. 1915 during the Panama International Exposition, and thus complete the greatest trip ever known.

C. C. BECK   J. B. RANSOM

THE OVERLAND WESTERNERS

G. W. BECK   R. G. RAYNE

A Pack Horse (Pinto)
and a Watch Dog (Nip)
Have undertaken a 20,000 mile overland trip.
With the proper care, this flag we'll bear.
Thru every State to the gates of the Frisco Fair.

event gave the visitor an interesting choice of souvenirs, and distribution by mail of these cards helped to popularise further the exciting hobby of deltiology. Picture postcards are still popular souvenir items wherever international fairs and expositions are held. Collectors should remember that issues representing a once-in-a-lifetime event will always increase in interest and value.

As a promotion for the 1915 San Francisco Exposition four men travelled on pack horses through every state in the U.S. This double postcard (above and right) recorded the event.

66

7

Greeting Cards

While the picture postcard might have been a relatively new invention in the late nineteenth century, greeting cards, especially valentines, were used in England as early as 1667. It was then that Samuel Pepys wrote, 'This morning came to my bedside (I being up dressing myself) little Will Mercer to be her Valentine; and he brought her name writ upon blue paper in gold letters, very pretty; and we were both well pleased with it'. It wasn't until the end of the eighteenth century that valentines and other printed paper greetings were commercially produced for those who found it easier to let someone else speak for them when it came to declaring a sentimental message.

Christmas cards and valentines were the earliest of commercially manufactured cards and the nineteenth century saw the emergence of elaborate paper declarations of undying love. These were often arranged bits of paper lace, foil paper and highly glazed embossed flowers and ribbons. These replaced the single sheet of paper used in the eighteenth century. The early greetings were copperplate engraved until about 1830 when lithography came into general use. With the advent of the penny-post and the halfpenny rate in England for cards in 1875 the sending of greeting cards was already well established as a national custom. Over one and a half million such cards had gone through the post in Great Britain in 1870.

After the elaborate greeting cards that preceded the general use of the penny postcard, it took a great deal of ingenuity on the part of the designers to get all of the elements of earlier cards that could be protected by an envelope onto an unprotected small piece of cardboard that would get much handling before it reached its destination. The ways in which this problem was solved were remarkable. The more elaborate greeting cards were continued to be made, but the immediate popularity of the picture postcard led to the use of the flat card with nothing more than an artist's illustration and a short message.

The greeting card, in essence, had come full circle, from a large piece of paper with an illustration and a message to a small piece of cardboard with the same elements. This is not to say that ingenious postcard manufacturers did not manage to make cards that contained all of the elements of the enveloped variety. They did. Folded accordion tissue paper and gilt foil as well as many other applied materials and novelty designs adapted from the earlier greeting cards were used. But for the most part, the colorful picture postcard sent to greet a loved one on a special holiday provided work for thousands of artists during the golden age.

It eventually became the custom to send cards, not only on Valentine's Day and Christmas, but on birthdays, Easter, New

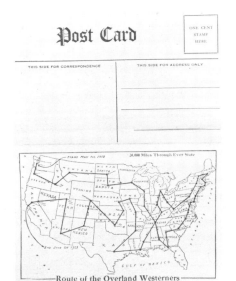

67

From the Paris Exposition of 1900, with insert of color transparency.

Angels adorned many Christmas greeting postcards. Brightly lithographed cards were embossed and gilded.

Framed scenes within greeting cards were popular. Many scenes were painted by established artists.

Bells were used as symbols of Christmas joy. Especially lovely are those with painted landscapes and Christmas or winter scenes.

A Christmas greeting postcard showing an early radio.

Souvenir de Paris

le 1900

Amitiés de

EDITEUR H. BAUER 15 RUE DE BONDY · PARIS · IMPORTÉ

Through branches green shine candles bright,

Heralding the Christmas night.

Huld's Puzzle Series No. 10-a.   Copyr., 1906, by Franz Huld, Pub., N. Y.

Never mind how cold the weather,

Christmas brings us close together.

Huld's Puzzle Series No. 10-b.   Copyr., 1906, by Franz Huld, Pub., N. Y.

On my Third hangs many a Gingerbread man,

Get hold of as many as ever you can.

Huld's Puzzle Series No. 10-c.   Copyr., 1906, by Franz Huld, Pub., N. Y.

Your Christmas Tree I'm now completing,

Accept it, dear, with loving Greeting.

Huld's Puzzle Series No. 10-d.   Copyr., 1906, by Franz Huld, Pub., N. Y.

Installment Christmas card was sent over a period of four days and made up complete picture when all cards were received.

Proportionately few Easter greeting cards had religious motifs. These two have gold or silver foil backgrounds and decorative crosses.

Postcard sent from Rome at Easter with portrait of Pope.

Year's Day, St. Patrick's Day and even Leap Year. In America, national holidays such as Thanksgiving, the 4th of July, Washington's Birthday and the anniversary of the day on which Abraham Lincoln was born were all reasons to send colorful greetings. It almost seemed as though holidays were invented to increase the postcard business. April Fool's Day was also a day for sending and receiving greetings, many of them comic and some of them insulting.

For the deltiologist there is a wealth of interest among the early greeting postcards. Among these are the New Year's cards made during the first decade of this century with the year numbers fashioned from unusual figures or objects. The digits 1908 for instance can be found in the guise of snowmen with top hats. Another card for that year has the numbers outlined by children dressed in delightful winter costumes.

New Year's Day cards for French and German markets have symbols of good luck that seem to have been indigenous to those countries: the pig holding satchels of coins, the four-leaf clover, ladybugs, mushrooms and the swastika can all be found. It is probably not generally known, except among postcard collectors, that the swastika was once considered a good-luck symbol.

71

Two New Year greeting cards with clocks as motifs.

German New Year greetings depict the pig as a symbol of good luck. Four-leaf clovers, coins, ladybugs, mushrooms and the swastika were other symbols of luck.

Jewish New Year cards were simply stock greeting cards overprinted with a New Year wish in Hebrew.

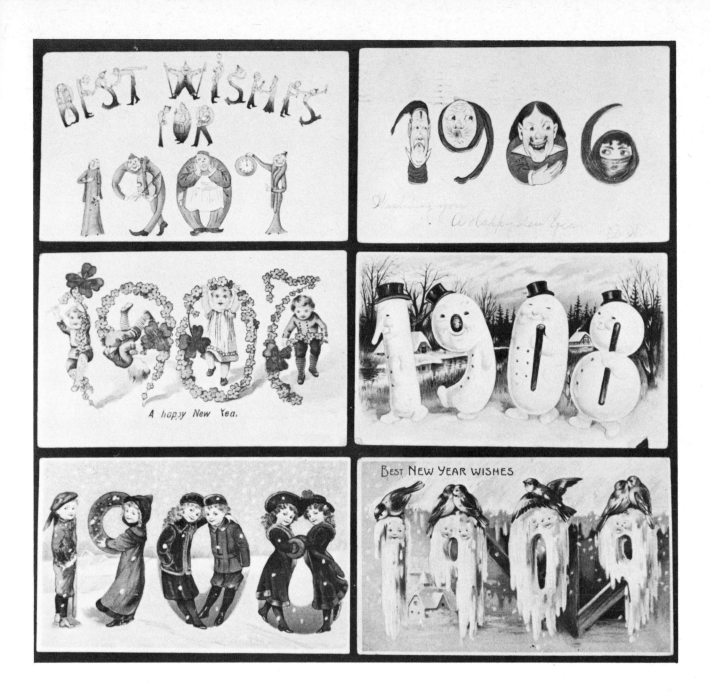

Unusual methods of depicting year numbers on New Year greeting postcards seemed to be popular for a few years.

Many of the more prolific picture postcard artists designed cards in quantity for every holiday and these were issued over a period of years if they proved to be popular. Ellen H. Clapsaddle designed especially charming groups of valentines and it is probable that she wrote many of the sayings and verses for them as well as painted the original designs. One rather amusing limerick appears on a Clapsaddle valentine:

> There was a young lady who couldn't
> Endure anything that she shouldn't;
> Her halo was bright
> And it fitted just right.
> Would you think she would please? –
> No, she wouldn't.

More sentimental Clapsaddle cards bore messages such as 'All that's sweet, by love's decree, Has been made resembling thee.'

German Christmas cards show angels with enormous embossed and gilded wings and cherubic winged children. There are frequently motifs of music or musical instruments such as organs,

73

Valentine greetings with blacks as subjects were anything but 'loving thoughts' to an oppressed race.

Embossed brightly lithographed Valentine postcards made in Germany.

Leap Year cards are less common than most greeting postcards. These are from etchings and the heart is printed in red.

74

Birthday greetings with flowers were simple and beautiful.

bells, violins or lutes included in the pictures. Identical cards can be found with the message printed in a variety of languages. 'Froliche Weinachten' or 'Merry Christmas' are found on cards of the same design and manufacture, proving once again that the greeting postcard business was truly an international one.

As is pointed out in another chapter, the evolution of Santa Claus as a symbol of Christmas can be traced on the cards made in the first fifteen years of this century. Santa's attire as seen on the earliest Christmas greeting postcards is more ecclesiastical than what we have come to accept as the traditional 'St. Nick.' However, he is always carrying a bag of toys and is usually surrounded by happy children.

Elaborate bells with Christmas winter scenes on them were frequently used as symbols on Christmas cards. Boughs of holly and pieces of mistletoe sometimes surround the bells and the messages above or below are short and simple; 'Joyful Christmas', 'Christmas Greeting', or 'With Best Christmas Wishes' did not require any creativity on the part of the writer.

Of particular interest to American collectors are the novelty 'Thanksgiving Menu' cards. Some of these relayed appropriate toasts for the feast day such as 'May you enlarge your waist, By humoring your taste' and the menu was for real food traditional on the holiday. Other 'Menu' cards wished the recipient 'Good luck, Success, Riches garnished with Good Health and Long Life alla spirit consolation'. The menus were fictional.

A great many Leap Year cards were produced considering the limited market for such greetings. The holiday seems to have been taken somewhat more seriously in those days before women's liberation. Many of these cards were comic, but some of those illustrated here show etchings of rather winsome ladies and messages such as, 'I'll get you yet,' and 'Four years I've waited. You will now be mine'. Since these were a series titled 'Leap year Thoughts', it is probable that these sentiments were never uttered aloud and the card had to suffice to get the message across. One wonders at the amount that were probably sent out unsigned, therefore defeating their purpose.

Thanksgiving Day 'menu' cards.

76

The turkey became, dead or alive, a symbol for Thanksgiving, and postcards were exchanged on that American holiday.

Many Easter cards were designed and a lot of these were made to appeal especially to children. Chubby children's faces emerge from chicken eggs, children are depicted in bunny costumes and are usually carrying or looking for colorful Easter eggs.

Relatively few religious cards were printed for either Christmas or Easter and it is probable that there are fewer picture postcards with religious motifs for collectors than many other categories of greeting cards. Jewish New Year cards were designed and published that had greetings in Hebrew and English. Many of the designs, however, have no religious symbolism on them and flowers and children were used instead. On some Easter cards crosses of flowers were used, but unlike modern Christmas and Easter greeting cards, there seems to be little use of other religious symbols that were reserved for Sunday school reward cards.

For deltiologists, 'greeting' cards as a category for collecting includes all of those 'special day' issues to commemorate holidays in many countries. These were the forerunners of modern day greeting cards that are once again put into envelopes and mailed at letter rates. The history of the greeting card has come full circle, but for a short quarter of a century the beautifully lithographed, gilded and embossed picture postcards carried messages of good wishes for many special holidays throughout the world.

77

8

Children on Postcards

Artists who were capable of painting children in charming poses were in high demand as postcard illustrators. Many of the artists who became well known as specialists in drawing and painting juvenile subjects were highly successful and were popular during the first picture postcard collecting boom. These same cards are even more desirable now. The cards of Mabel Lucie Atwell, Kate Greenaway, Ellen H. Clapsaddle, Jennie Harbour, Florence Hardy, Mortimer Menpes and many others are extremely popular with modern collectors and prices for some of the cards by these artists have soared in the past few years.

Rose O'Neill cards illustrated with her famous Kewpies are highly collectible today. Many of these are Christmas greeting cards and depict the Kewpies in a variety of holiday scenes.

Children became the subjects of many advertising cards and many became trade-marks of their companies. Especially attractive children were photographed in rather saccharine poses. For these photographed cards, curly hair was always a must and there were obviously more blonde models in demand than brunettes. Cards thought to be somewhat naughty for the time show the child model sitting on the potty or in the bath and thousands of tykes must have caught colds as photographers had them posing without clothing in many situations. Poses that would have been degrading and far from amusing had the subjects been adults were considered all right if the models were chubby young nude or semi-nude children. Often the titles under these pictures had double meanings.

Opposite.
1st row: three cards of series, 'Baby's Habits'.
2nd row: a group of postcards showing stork delivering babies. These were used as birth announcements.
3rd row: babies in military garb and national 'costumes' were popular subjects.

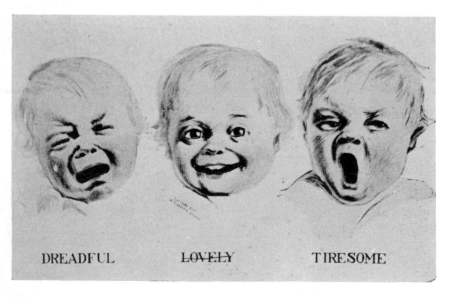

DREADFUL   LOVELY   TIRESOME

Sender of this was obviously not fond of babies at that moment. Card is double weight and printed in U.S. by M. T. Sheahan, Boston, Mass.

78

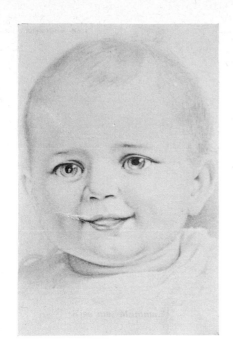

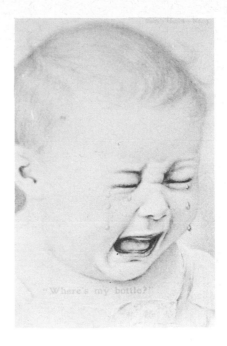

"Where's my bottle?"

Before the Bath.

GERMANY

SCOTLAND

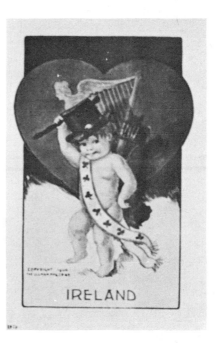

IRELAND

There were many infant cards, some of them charmingly painted. Birth announcement cards showing the mythical storks delivering the infants were very popular and there are some of this type that even have the stork delivering twins.

There were several series of cards showing children dressed in adult costume and pursuing adult occupations. One such series shows small boys as a baker, a blacksmith, a doctor, a lawyer, a carpenter and a railroad conductor. E. P. Kinsella painted a rather elphin little boy playing cricket. Katherine Gassaway children were large-eyed charmers in adorable poses. These cards were usually captioned.

Pretty little girls were painted in costumes adapted from flowers and each card was named by the flower the costume represented. Flowers and children were often used together and many times infants' or little girls' faces were painted as the centre of flowers.

Sunbonnet babies were popular subjects and while it is thought that Bertha L. Corbett was the first artist to design these charming cards, the idea was quickly taken up by other artists. Miss Corbett worked for the J. I. Austen Co. of Chicago and her idea in drawing the sunbonnet babies was that personality and charm could be depicted in children's figures without using any facial features. The Ullman Manufacturing Company of New York issued a series of sunbonnets drawn by Dorothy Dixon which some

Children as drawn by artist Florence Hardy.

80

The Singer.

Good Night

Good Morning

The Would-be sport.

Don't be afraid I'm here.

"Poor Things They'll get drowned."

Artist Katherine Gassaway painted charming wide-eyed children for the Rotograph Company, N.Y.

postcard historians think might have been a pseudonym for Bertha Corbett. Later Ullman sunbonnet baby cards were designed by Dr. Bernhardt Wall and some of these are signed. About seventy or more designs of sunbonnets exist that were popular between 1904 and 1912. The cards have once again become popular and their value has increased in the past couple of years.

The sunbonnet babies solved a major problem for the artists who painted them. They did not need a child model to paint the little flared dresses and the wide-brimmed bonnets that completely hid all facial features. Many of the sunbonnet babies are shown doing adult work and these cards were popular ones for adults to send to children since they pointed a moral.

Children often appeared as subjects of Easter postcards, and many show small children together with animals. Others show the children in animal costumes. These rabbits and chickens with small human faces made charming subjects for Easter greeting cards which were usually gilded, embossed and highly colored.

81

Fresh Rolls

The Village Blacksmith

A Decided Improvement

Now, Gentlemen of the Jury

The Handy Craftsman

On Time! at last

I luvis yo deah, and dat am why
I got him tho he roosted high

"Sweethearts."

I luvis yo deah wid my heart's whole power,
And feel jus as happy as a big sunflower.

82

Little children were often dressed in adult clothing or shown carrying on adult occupations. Note written by sender on center right-hand card illustrates that train schedules have always been a cause of frustration.

AFTER THE DIP!

H·DIX·SANDFORD

"Oilette"

If black children were thought to be good subjects, undressed black children were considered even funnier. This Tuck Oilette painted by Sandford is typical of the black 'put-down' postcard of the early part of this century.

Black children were often shown by the artist as barefoot and large-eyed and frequently all children on one card looked alike. Verses are always written in stereotype minstrel-show dialect.

It should come as no surprise that many Christmas cards were designed with children as the subjects. Many of these show boys and girls in contemporary costume playing around the Yule tree with the sort of toys that any wealthy child would expect to be given for Christmas around the turn of the century. These cards should be of interest to toy collectors since early electric trains and model automobiles as well as dolls and doll houses and rocking horses of the period can be seen on them. Other Christmas greeting cards show good little children being rewarded by a rather benevolent looking Father Christmas or Santa Claus. It is interesting that at the turn of the century there was not one figure that stood for Santa Claus. He can be seen as a tall, thin bishop or a grandfatherly bearded figure in a fur-trimmed red coat and pointed hat. It takes many years for the world to get a clear picture of a mythical folk character and it is obvious that the popularity of greeting postcards in this century has led to the evolvement of the stereotype Santa Claus. From the tall thin

83

AND DAD SAID "BE A MAN"

Wartime example showing wide-eyed child dressed as a soldier.

Early Detroit Publishing Company photographic cards are important documents of what people and places in the United States looked like in late nineteenth and early part of twentieth centuries. These are Ute Indian children photographed before 1899.

84

Advertising postcards that are considered completely offensive today were popular for albums when first issued by the Korn-Kinks Company at the beginning of this century.

stern-looking man in the jewelled white costume who carried a long staff to the rotund white-bearded jolly Santa we can see on picture postcards made for Christmas greetings the development of the mythical character who still brings the goodies on the Yuletide holiday.

Jenny Nystrom painted rather whimsical children, elves and animals and many of these are shown in situations that celebrate the Christmas season. Crying or smiling babies have always had appeal for artists and there are many cards showing babies in these poses. A series of infants called 'Baby's Habits' was especially popular. The beginning of World War I brought on many series of babies dressed in uniforms of the various countries. One particularly charming earlier card of this type shows an infant dressed in the 'Rough Rider' hat and the glasses that Theodore Roosevelt wore. In character with the man he is supposed to be representing, the child is smiling and showing his front teeth.

Later, war postcards were issued to raise money for 'the fatherless children of France' and were issued by an organisation of that name in New York as Christmas cards to raise money for that charity in the same way the United Nations Christmas cards are sold today. One of the French war orphan cards, painted by Walter St. Marie, shows a charitable American doughboy delivering gifts to French war orphans and another shows a young boy staring into a fireplace in the living room of the bombed-out building in which he has made his home. An empty stocking is hanging over the fireplace.

There were hundreds of artists who designed cards with children as the subjects and as was the case in the music halls of the period, adorable children and especially a child with a dog or other appealing animal, couldn't miss on the postcard market.

In addition to those cards using children as subjects, there were many made for children. Some of these were simple cut-outs such as paper dolls with a few changes of clothing, Punch and Judy shows or pictures of flowering plants that could be folded into three-dimensional dollhouse toys. These were often sent as inexpensive remembrances for children on birthdays or other holidays.

85

The Christmas Dinner

Children's Christmas Letter Story

By Charlotte Dodge Brombacher.

Miss Ethel Johnson,
Winchester,
N. H.

COPYRIGHT 1904 BY WALTER WIRTHS N.Y.

Folding three-part postcard is one of group of 'letter stories' made for children around 1904. The brightly colored card was issued by Walter Wirths of New York.

Instalment cards were especially charming gifts to send to children. A child would have the mail to look forward to for at least three days following the receipt of the first card, and when all were received, they were put together to form a picture. Very few of the cut-out cards or complete sets of instalment cards still survive and these, when they can be found in good condition, are very much in demand by today's collectors.

The costumes, hairstyles and children's toys of the beginning of this century are all documented on picture postcards. Children had their own postcard albums and collections to which doting relatives continually added. The messages written on these cards are often very revealing as to the kind of relationship parents and other adults had with their children during the early part of the century. 'Be a good girl' is often written. Other messages frequently seen are, 'Mother and Father will be back in five weeks', 'Be a good little girl for Nanny,' or 'Father comes here every day' (on a card showing a golf course in Bermuda).

86

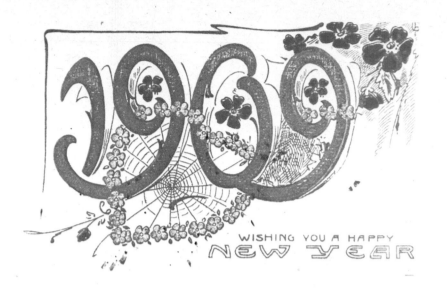

Hand-painted oriental postcard on bamboo paper.

Top left. Innovative letter and number styles were devised by artists responsible for thousands of new designs for greeting cards.

Centre and bottom left. Pair of St. Patrick's Day postcards with the symbols of harp and shamrocks.

Automobiles figure as motifs in thousands of greeting cards.

9

Animals on Postcards

If children were depicted as chickens and rabbits on Easter greeting cards there were many more animals on picture postcards that were shown in human poses. Many postcard publishers could have prophesied the popularity of Mickey Mouse, Donald Duck and other Walt Disney animal characters. Their issues of frogs, mice, chickens, cats, dogs, pigs and other forms of animal life were highly successful as postcard art. The animals, as in the Disney cartoons, were usually dressed in human clothing and many of them are shown engaging in human activities. Singing frogs, dressed in striped and polka-dotted shorts, must have amused many children who received these cards and cute mice in various situations of peril to life and limb most certainly prophesy the success of the Disney studios.

Dog lovers have thousands of picture postcards with their favorite subjects from which to choose. Many of the dog subject postcards were copies of paintings of the various breeds and were issued in sets for placement in albums. The paintings of dogs shown in noble poses were extremely popular.

Photographic poses of dogs were also items that enjoyed immense popularity. Frequently the poor animals were dressed in blouses, hats, collars and ties and photographed in poses that presupposed their human qualities. The miracle, of course, was that the photographers were able to get the animals to sit for their portraits in uncomfortable restrictive clothing and undoglike attitudes. Probably many of the dogs used for these cards were the animals that worked in vaudeville and music halls during the period preceding World War I.

There were no laws to protect children from long sittings at photographers at the time, much less animals, and if the results were amusing and attractive the cards made from these pictures would sell by the thousands.

If one dog as the subject of a photograph or painting to be used on a picture postcard was appealing, more dogs in one picture was a sure winner. There are many cards showing bitches of many breeds, some of questionable parentage, with their litters. Other cards showed groups of puppies in baskets or other receptacles. One bit of evidence that there was some concern for the welfare of animals is a card showing a particularly appealing puppy of no special breed looking soulfully through a wire fence over which is a sign, CITY POUND. The caption on the bottom of this card, which was painted by V. Colby, is, 'I don't want to be an angel!' Since there were so many cards made with dogs as subjects, few of these have become very high-priced as yet. How-

Top – left: general greeting card in art nouveau style. Note inset of peacock feather design. Center: this early greeting card for Thanksgiving by International Art might be a Clapsaddle design; it is unsigned. Right: charming item entitled 'The Critic' shows small boy drawing with chalk. Bottom: flat planes and dark outlines in designs for these cards made them especially adaptable to the art of lithography.

89

MONKEY

LION

FOX

OPOSSUM

CAMEL

ELEPHANT

Hundreds of animal series were issued for albums. These are by Tuck.

"Jappy and Happy"   Louis Wain.

An example of Louis Wain cats acting like humans.

162—A Temperance Outfit.

Pack mules of the American West with contemporary caption concerning Temperance movement.

ever, as the supply becomes shorter prices are destined to rise.

There are dog lovers and there are cat lovers and those enamored of cats were not neglected when they chose picture postcards to send to friends or to insert in their albums. Raphael Tuck printed many series with feline portraits. Three series with cat subjects by Tuck were 'Kittendom,' 'Animal Life,' and 'Humorous Cats'.

Louis Wain was an artist who specialised in cat paintings which were reproduced by Tuck. Wain's cats were black, orange striped or common alley cats and are usually shown doing human things. Wain began his career as an illustrator of animals for books and around 1900 he began to paint cats for picture postcards. He eventually sold his work to many publishers but the bulk of his work was done for Tuck. He also painted for Faulkner and Davidson Brothers. His cats look more like people than cats, are usually dressed and appear in human situations. The Wain cards are mostly captioned and signed by the artist.

At first, just accessories were used to dress the Wain cats, but as time went on the cats were more completely clothed and the situations were totally human. A series for Tuck called 'Louis Wain's Cats' show the animals as real cats except that they all have human qualities in the expressions.

Photographic postcards of cats or dogs doing tricks or dressed as humans were extremely popular.

91

92

Top: Australian animal series were welcome additions to postcard albums.
Bottom: series of Australian birds was published in Sydney.

Opposite.
1st row: dogs portrayed as noble beasts were always popular; these are all lithographs from portraits.
2nd row: colorful lepidopteral postcards have the names of the illustrated specimens printed on reverse side.
3rd row: underwater animals were popular album subjects.

Cat photography was popular as postcard subjects and the Rotograph Company of New York and C. E. Bullard issued cards of cats and kittens photographed in black and white, dressed or undressed and sitting in any available receptacle. The photographer, Landor, sold cat photographs to Tuck, Hartmann and Wrench. His photographs were always captioned in a manner that gave the cats a human quality. Accessories and props also lent a kind of humanisation to the animals.

Besides cats and dogs, other domestic and barnyard animals were used as subjects on picture postcards. The pig, a symbol of good luck to Germans and other Europeans, was used as the subject of thousands of New Year greetings. The New Year pig usually is shown painted in comic character. He is sometimes dressed in human clothing and sometimes not, but he is always depicted as a humanised character. Cards of American manufacture often used pigs for illustrations, but the pig in any aspect on these cards is always treated humorously. One photographic

card of three suckling pigs and their mother is captioned, 'A lot of suckers in Pittsburgh, Pa'. Another card has a drawing of a cow suckling two piglets and the caption, 'The Lord helps those who help themselves'.

Just about every animal known to man was the subject of more than one picture postcard. Tuck issued many series of album cards with animals as the motif. 'Wild Animals' and 'Domestic Animals' as well as undersea and bird life were series of cards issued by Tuck.

Buffalos, yaks, zebras, giraffes, tigers, elephants, mules, camels, sheep and hundreds of other animals were both painted and photographed for cards that would be bought to complete postcard album menageries. In demand by collectors especially were esoteric animals of foreign lands. Examples of these are the birds and animals of Australia illustrated on the previous page. Photographic postcards of circus animals were also very popular. Exotic birds in bright plumage were welcome additions to most postcard albums as were butterflies, insects and fish.

Domestic wildlife was used often on picture postcards and the turkey naturally became the most popular symbol for American Thanksgiving cards. The horse and wagon is often depicted and of special interest to collectors of cards of the American West are those showing pack mules in various situations, some of them humorous. Birds of all varieties decorate many greeting cards.

Had animals been ignored as subjects of picture postcards many of the most beautiful and charming collectors' items would not exist today. So many were made that it is possible to build extensive collections by specialising in horses, dogs or cats. One could collect Louis Wain's cards of cat drawings and fill many albums or files. Anyone specialising in Tuck's animal series could spend a lifetime filling in sets. The postcard designer's ingenuity, when it came to adapting our furry or feathered friends, was unlimited.

In the days before television the circus held a lot of excitement and glamor.

94

10

Comic and Macabre

A typical joke of a popular stand-up comedian is the one-liner, 'Take my wife . . . *Please!*' Unfortunately, this is the caliber of humor of many of the comic postcards that were extremely popular at the turn of the century. Not only wives, but mothers-in-law, sons-in-law, the hen-pecked husband, old maids and various ethnic groups such as blacks and orientals were the brunt of the thousands of comic cards published during the first period of postcard collecting. Minor subjects were the Suffragette movement (the women retaliated with propaganda cards of their own); facial hair on men. ('How to get used to a moustache: Dip a hairbrush in brilliantine and rub gently on the lips'.) The drunk and drinking were subjects that were covered fully by the British humorists.

One especially typical mother-in-law card has the legend, 'So my daughter's husband says he'll put me out of the house, does he? Well, we shall see; Here I am and here I will remain to protect my poor girl'. A variation of the mother-in-law card, appropriate for the mother of the groom reads, 'Hoity, toity! Because a lady is a little plump, is she to be sneered at by her own son's wife, who is all skin and bone? But I will protect my boy in spite of her'. Obviously, a great deal of hostility could be vented by sending one of these cards to the appropriate person. The drawings of ugly, large-headed women on this type of card are especially vicious. Mothers-in-law at the end of the nineteenth century were often depicted as sub-human by the British cartoonists.

The hen-pecked husband did not fare much better at the hands of the British humorists. One card has an illustration of the husband on his knees with his hands in a clasped position and the legend reads, 'I have put the babies to bed, my love; may I now go out for a walk?' One look at the wife's ugly face convinces the reader that the poor man's wish would not be granted. Another card shows the wife beating her husband and the card reads, 'I'll teach you to wink at Mrs. Harris! Wink at that – and that!' Any woman who received one of these cards, probably unsigned, might have had serious doubts about the stability of her marriage. However, it is doubtful that these cards were sent often to convey the messages they carried to those who might deserve them. It is more likely that they were printed mainly as cartoons to be inserted in the family postcard album to be chuckled over on a quiet winter evening.

While the artists who specialised in humor are noted in the chapter on signed picture postcards, it should be mentioned here

Women's suffrage was the butt of many comic cards of the beginning of this century.

Will those in favour of Women's Suffrage please hold up their hands?"

95

How to get used to kissing a moustache :—
"Dip a hair-brush in brilliantine and rub gently on the lips."

Above left and center, and left: mother-in-law jokes were favorite music hall humor and many comic cards used this theme.

Above right: Edwardian moustaches were often a source of amusement.

Bottom: the hen-pecked husband was thought to be an hilarious subject.

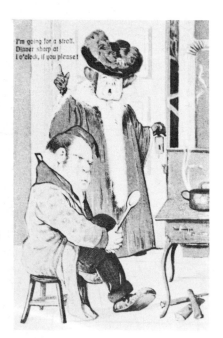

96

Let not the Right Hand know what the
Left Hand doeth.

A SCOTCH REEL (WITH REAL SCOTCH)

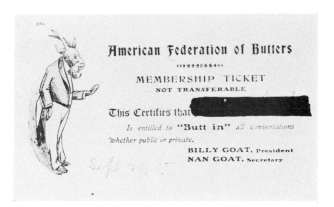

American Federation of Butters

MEMBERSHIP TICKET
NOT TRANSFERABLE

This Certifies that

Is entitled to "Butt in" all conversations
whether public or private.

BILLY GOAT, President
NAN GOAT, Secretary

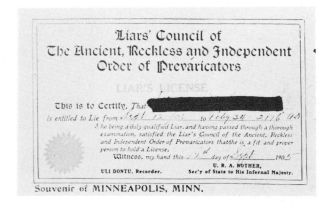

Liars' Council of
The Ancient, Reckless and Independent
Order of Prevaricators

LIAR'S LICENSE

This is to Certify, That
is entitled to Lie from Sept 12 05 to Feby 34 2176 05
She being a duly qualified Liar, and having passed through a thorough
examination, satisfied the Liar's Council of the Ancient, Reckless
and Independent Order of Prevaricators thatshe is, a fit and proper
person to hold a License.
Witness, my hand this 12th day of Sept 1905

ULI DONTU, Recorder.
U. R. A. MOTHER,
Sec'y of State to His Infernal Majesty.

Souvenir of MINNEAPOLIS, MINN.

Top: drinking was also a favorite subject for British and American humorists. Bottom: two examples from a group of cards that were thought to be funny at the turn of the century and after.

that many of the British postcard artists were leading cartoonists for the magazine, *Punch*. The humor of the period leading to World War I might elude us now, but there were thousands of these cartoon cards printed and they were undoubtedly popular in their time.

Drunks and excessive imbibing were often subjects for cards that had New Year greetings. 'The morning after' was a subject and was popular in the United States and England where neither country takes precedence for its number of alcoholics in proportion to its population. Drunks are shown suffering all the evils of hangover that an artist could, in any sober moment, conjure.

Cartoons appropriate to vacationers were rather daring for the time. Many of them show women in what were considered rather revealing bathing costumes being pinched and flirted with by men in bathing trunks. Other vacationers, if they thought these cards too risqué to send through the post could purchase Donald McGill cards showing the hotels as being so crowded that the sender supposedly had to sleep on the roof. ('I'm taking pot luck – in tip-top digs.') Still other humorous cards poke fun at that now popular means of transportation, the automobile.

Along with the above subjects, the cartoonist postcard designers did not forget the avid postcard collectors as subjects for a jibe or two. There are to be found today many postcards made during the craze for collecting that poke fun at the hobby and the many thousands who indulged in it. The Arthur Gill card

97

DOSE ANGELS.

Vimen, ven she dakes her ease,
Vas auful queer und hardt to please;
But ven bad troubles calls us down,
She charmes avay dot angry frown;
Mit ice-cream hands
She warms der pain -
Raise high der stein to her again!

To Vimmin

I trink der health
of Vomen-kind,
For her mine heart
vas friend-vise;
But ven she did
excited git -
She talks so fast,
your chance vas NIT
To git ein vord
in end-vise :
But den dot lonesomeness so queer,
If doze shweet voices vasn't here.

Some Advices

So higher as two kites we see
Dot good old toast unfurled,
Der hand vot rocks der cradle,
Iss der hand dot rocks der vorld,
But look aout, poys,
or may be, too,
You'll haf dot hand a'rockin' you

To Dose Better Hafs

Trink to der frau who vorks by dot store,
Helping along der peezness some more;
Cutting head cheezes und nice peef-steaks,
Sauer-krout, pickels und pigs-feet makes;
By shiminy gracious
Dis vorld mit out
Dose petter-haf voomens, voud go, -
"Oup der Spout."

THE TOAST

"May old Dame Fortune smile
her most beneficent smiles,
and may her daughter Miss Fortune
never darken your door or cast a
passing shadow over your hearth."

To Vimmins

I raise mein stein
to Voman-kind,
Und makes dis
leetle jokes,
She vas der clingin'
vine so veak,
Und we der
sturdy Oaks;
But ven in bed
so sick ve lay,
Ah, ha! Twas youst de oder way.

Seaside scenes were considered humorous and daring at turn of the century.

I'm taking pot luck - in tip-top digs.

A Donald McGill postcard sold at vacation resorts.

MONK. "HULLO, TIGE! COLLECTIN' PICTURE POSTCARDS?"
TIGER. "NOPE! COLLECTIN' COLLECTORS!"

Arthur Gill cartoon poking fun at the thousands of postcard collectors before World War I.

Opposite – center and bottom rows: 'toasts' in German dialect were considered humorous. In contrast, card at bottom center is 'philosophical'.

included here is only one example, but certainly a typical one.

One peculiar type of humorous card can be found in the insulting 'membership' postcards that seem to have been filled out with the name of the recipient, but like many other 'put-down' cards, are not signed by the sender. There seem to have been more of these made for the American market than for other countries. One card entitles the bearer to 'butt in' on all conversations, whether public or private. Another admits the recipient membership in the 'Liars' Council of the Ancient, Reckless and Independent Order of Prevaricators'. This was certainly a far from flattering souvenir to send anyone from Minneapolis, Minnesota, or, indeed, anywhere else in the world. A card with two jack-asses facing each other and the message, 'When shall we three meet again?' is self-explanatory and leads one to think that the recipient would either have had to have been a very good friend or a very real enemy not to have been insulted by the receipt of such a card.

Foreign dialect was evidently thought to be a cause for hilarity in the late nineteenth century and adult as well as children's cards were printed with the verse or greeting in German or Dutch dialect. Cards with blacks as subjects also

99

LE PLUS ANCIEN BOURGEOIS DE BRUXELLES.

COPYRIGHTED L'EDITION D'ART BRUXELLES

MANNEKEN - PIS EN GARDE CIVIQUE.

COPYRIGHTED L'EDITION D'ART BRUXELLES

MANNEKEN - PIS EN GÉNÉRAL.

COPYRIGHTED L'EDITION D'ART BRUXELLES

Another proof of Darwin's theory

100

A HAS BEEN

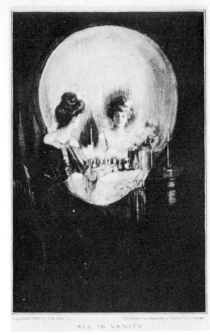

ALL IS VANITY

Opposite left, and bottom left: revolving disc card was probably considered hilarious in its time. Bathroom humor is no longer popular.

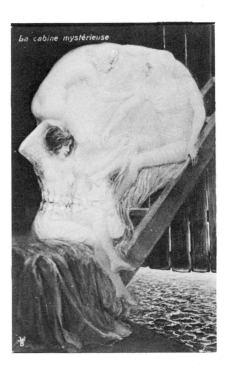

La cabine mystérieuse

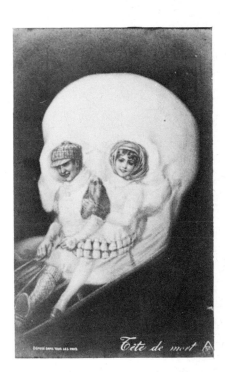

Tête de mort

Illustrating interesting style of macabre decadent art.

Left: self-explanatory postcard poking fun of resemblance between man and fish.

were printed in a dialect assumed to be 'the way they talk'. Puns were used frequently on comic cards and drawings used in the place of words were a common technique of combining the medium with the message.

If we find the postcards of an earlier period less humorous than our ancestors of seventy or eighty years ago seemed to find them, perhaps it is because so much of what was once called 'funny' seems only insulting today. There is certainly more sensitivity to the problems of minority groups; sex is now a subject that is no longer a cause for snickering; and few husbands stay around long enough to consider themselves 'hen-pecked'. In addition, bathroom humor, such as that shown in the moveable disc card of French manufacture illustrated here, is simply not funny any longer. One no longer laughs at the many stereotypes that were the cause of hilarity in burlesque houses and British music halls and that were carried over to the comic postcards of the late

101

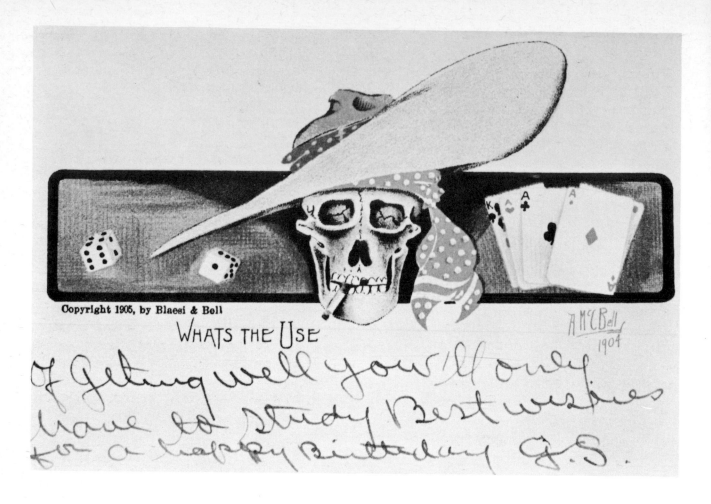

Copyright 1905, by Blaesi & Bell

WHATS THE USE

A M C Bell
1904

Of getting well you'll only have to study Best wishes for a happy Birthday G.S.

nineteenth and early twentieth centuries. However, to historians of the evolution of humor there is no better record of what made people laugh during the Edwardian period than the thousands of picture postcards that still exist.

If there were cards to make one laugh, there were also a few that were designed to make one shudder. An assortment of cards in the style of decadent art were designed at the turn of the century on the Continent that were exported to England and America and these evidently enjoyed a rather large sale.

The majority of these macabre cards have as their major motif rather grizzly skulls which, upon further examination, contain pictures within pictures of innocent children or less innocent men and women. All have a 'death is imminent' theme and were printed in black and white. The heads of the figures within usually form eyes of the skull and the captions are as frightening as the drawings. One grinning skull which contains an inner drawing of two children on a sled is called, 'tete de mort'.

Another skull turns out, on closer examination, to be a picture of a beautiful young woman looking into her mirror and the legend, 'All is vanity', certainly gives one pause.

Other less artistic macabre postcards were designed to illustrate the inevitability of death and the skull is arranged in the drawing with poker chips and playing cards to illustrate that life is a gamble. 'A game of chance' is the title of one such card. One young sender, however, was able to put the macabre subjects of skull, dice and playing cards in their proper perspective. Having sent the frightening card to a friend who was obviously sick (in itself, something to ponder over) the sender added to the printed 'Write-away' message, 'What's the use', the additional words, . . . 'of getting well, you'll only have to study'.

The futility of life was summed up by young sender of this card.

102

11

Transportation

The end of the nineteenth century was an exciting period in the history of transportation and the postcard publishers did not avoid their responsibility in recording every new invention that would carry man into the air, provide luxury on the sea or get him from one place to another on any number of wheels.

Man had long dreamed of flying like the birds and the first recorded attempt to fly is told in the Greek legend of Icarus whose father, Daedalus, made wings of feathers and wax in order to escape imprisonment in the labyrinth of Crete. Daedalus escaped, but Icarus, in his boyish exuberance, flew too close to the sun and plunged to his death when the wax melted. Unfortunately, no postcards were made to record that flight. Leonardo da Vinci's early attempts to fly also go unrecorded. However, just about every other flying machine that was invented at later dates, mainly at the end of the nineteenth century, were subjects for picture postcards, whether they actually got off the ground or not. If one did manage to get his machine in the air and later crashed, that disastrous event caused the postcard publishers to go to press with a photograph since the market for cards showing disasters has always been great.

Sir George Cayley of Great Britain was the first man to devise several forms of aircraft in the early 1800s that were to lay the foundation for the invention of later machines with which we are concerned here; those that really worked and were in one piece long enough to be photographed or painted for postcard subjects. Cayley was the first to consider that workable aircraft could be heavier than air. Work on this theory was continued by William Henson and John Stringfellow; Henson by designing a small steam engine and Stringfellow by improving Hensen's design in 1842 in constructing a steam-driven model plane that could lift at least part of its weight.

In the second part of the nineteenth century experimentation with gliders continued and notable names in this area are the German, Otto Lilienthal, who constructed and flew his first glider in 1891, and others in England such as Percy S. Pilcher and John J. Montgomery.

Professor Samuel P. Langley, of the Smithsonian Institution, Washington, D.C., seems to have been the first to have designed a small unmanned airplane. This was a tandem-winged monoplane model with a one-horsepower steam engine and two propellors. In 1896 the Langley plane flew over half a mile. The first heavier-than-air craft was invented by Langley, but he abandoned his projects in 1903 when his first full-scale gasoline-engined monoplane failed to fly.

Orville and Wilbur Wright were successful in getting their first controlled, powered flight of a heavier-than-air machine off

·FLYING·TAUGHT·BY·MALE·

·THE·SAME·OLD·PILOT·

En Stockholmsutflykt

Kongl. Slottet

Axel Eliassons Konstförlag, Stockholm. 2583

En Stockholmsutflykt

Strömparterren

Axel Eliassons Konstförlag, Stockholm. 2586

104

The airplane figured in these cartoon-type postcards.

SESQUI-CENTENNIAL INTERNATIONAL EXPOSITION, PHILADELPHIA, PA.

FOKKER THE SEVENTH, "TIMCOTOS" 1926,
USED IN COMMANDER BYRD'S FLIGHT OVER THE NORTH POLE.

Top: from sesqui-centennial International Exposition in Philadelphia showing plane, 'Fokker', from North Pole expedition. Bottom: riverboat excursions featured stops along the route for mailing postcards.

Travel by umbrella was not a common mode of getting from one place to another except in the mind of the publisher of these composite photographic postcards printed in Stockholm.

the ground and the postcard manufacturers on both sides of the Atlantic were quick to record that remarkable accomplishment. Just as today's collectors of modern postcards know that those cards commemorating rocket flights to the moon will be important documentation someday, so did the publishers rush the photographs of the new inventions in air travel into print for the avid collectors of their period.

The first officially witnessed airplane flight in Europe was made in 1906 by Alberto Santos-Dumont, a Brazilian, who flew six hundred feet in twenty-one seconds. Wilbur Wright made an uninterrupted flight of seventy-seven miles near Le Mans, France, in 1908 and in 1909 Louis Blériot was the first man to fly across the English Channel.

Another flying machine of sorts was devised by Count Ferdinand von Zeppelin whose large rigid airships had multiple balloon gas compartments. The dirigibles became known as 'zeppelins' and the German army officer-inventor became world famous. Zeppelin's first dirigible, Lu-1, flew on 2 July 1900, and stayed aloft for twenty minutes before it crashed. Zeppelin was able to build a reasonably successful model by 1908–9 through gifts of his friends and the German Government since he had used up his vast fortune in the earlier stages of development.

105

Ships and boats of all kinds are collected by those who specialize in that type of transportation postcard.

Dirigibles were used for bombing raids during World War I, but they were such easy targets for anti-aircraft guns that they had limited success. After the war, zeppelins were constructed for trans-oceanic transportation until the last, the *Hindenburg*, exploded over Lakehurst, N.J., in 1937. Although by this time deltiology was not the hobby it had once been, the event was duly recorded on many cards for those who 'collect disasters'.

106

The great ships that crossed the oceans and the smaller boats that traveled inland waters were all desired by collectors and are once again sought.

The period of luxurious ocean liner travel is also recorded on picture postcards. Many of the successful publishers reproduced paintings of ships. One series that is sought by collectors today was painted by Fred W. Leighton and is entitled 'Code Signals'. The signal flags flying above the ships are really messages such as 'all well' or 'shall I come?' that might be pertinent to someone sending a postcard message. Tuck also issued a series of ship paintings called 'Celebrated Liners'. All ships belonging to Great Britain were used as subjects for postcards and ships of many other countries were duly recorded in the same manner.

One interesting type of ship postcard was issued by the shipping lines, themselves, and given away to passengers once the ship got under way, The shiplines also pandered to the craze for postcard collecting by issuing menus, the top half of which could be cut off and mailed. A new one was issued each day. The sinking of the *Lusitania* put an end to the pre-World War I ocean voyages and the craze for picture postcards diminished at the same time. After that disastrous event, when the British transoceanic liner was sunk by a German submarine off Kinsale Head,

107

Ireland, on 7 May 1915, both the United States and Europe had other things besides postcards to concern themselves with.

The horseless carriage was another means of transportation that came into its own during the postcard collecting craze. The first lightweight serviceable steam automobile was built in 1897 by Francis and Freelan Stanley and by the 1880s electric automobiles were being made in Europe. America's earliest electric cars were built during the 1890s. Karl Benz and Gottlieb Daimler were the world's first manufacturers of internal combustion engine powered automobiles and the French engineer, Emile C. Lavassor designed an automobile in 1891 that was the prototype for many that were to follow.

The first commercially successful gasoline powered automobiles that were built in the United States were two-cylinder cars built by Charles E. and J. Frank Duryea of Massachusetts. In 1896 their company produced thirteen cars from the same plans and that same year Hansom E. Olds and Henry Ford built their first cars. Many others were to follow soon and the automobile was here to stay . . . and to have its development recorded on picture postcards. British humorists were quick to see the

Railroads as well as shipping lines advertised on picture postcards.

108

NOW THEN! DON'T GO TRYING TO GET UNDER THAT BUS;---WAIT YOUR TURN!

DRIVER "348 ACCIDENTS HAVE HAPPENED HERE--AN' ALL CAUSED THROUGH CARELESS DRIVING!"

Automobiles were a favorite humorous subject. Fortunately, the woman driver hadn't become enough of a factor at the time to be ridiculed.

Come away, my dears—perhaps it's a wrecked Zeppelin.

New methods of travel were a cause for the humorists to comment.

advantages for comic subjects in the gradual use of the automobile and often used inept drivers as the butt of their comedy. Jibes at women drivers did not, fortunately, occur to most of the cartoon artists at this early date.

Train buffs will find a wealth of railroad history on picture postcards. Especially in the United States, where railroad transportation is rapidly deteriorating, postcard collectors search for pictures of now defunct lines and engines that were at one time the only dependable mode of coast-to-coast transportation. If America had spent an entire century building a remarkable network of railroads, the postcard manufacturers spent almost twenty years recording it.

Other modes of transportation, from balloons to bicycles, trolleys, buses, and even pack animals can all be found as subjects of old picture postcards. In most cases collectors specialise in one mode of transportation such as trains, ocean liners or airplanes. Since most of these cards are actual photographs they present a rather accurate record of how people got from one place to another at the end of the last century and the beginning of this one.

109

12

Disaster and Natural Phenomena

Human fascination with disasters and natural phenomena is a fact that was recorded in great quantity and detail on picture postcards. Any disastrous event was a reason for cameramen to rush to the scene and record it, not only for local newspapers, but as a sure sale to the postcard publishers. Among the popular disasters were fires, unusually destructive storms or floods, shipwrecks, airplane or dirigible accidents, earthquakes and even trolley accidents.

Destruction by fire seemed to hold a special fascination for disaster collectors and not only fire scenes, themselves, but the brave men who fought the fires and the complicated and flashy equipment they used were duly recorded in action on picture postcards of the early twentieth century.

One can trace the development and improvement of fire-

Any disaster, large or small, was cause for postcards to be issued with either photographs or artist's impression of the happening.

110

Postcards showing fires and fire-fighting equipment have been collected continuously since the beginning of this century. The latest equipment was usually photographed for cards.

fighting equipment from the steam fire engines drawn by horses of the late 1800s to the gasoline powered pumpers of the early 1900s. All cities and towns knew from bitter experience that it was wise to invest in the latest in fire fighting equipment and they purchased the best and most modern they could afford. A disastrous fire had already struck the city of Chicago and smaller

111

GUERRE 1914-19'5
303. RAON-L'ETAPE (Vosges) — La Poste

à St-Dié   C. Cuny, éditeur, Saint-Dié

Far left and below: natural phenomena were often portrayed. Most of these were not actual photos of the events, however.

A World War I postcard.

TOTAL ECLIPSE OF THE SUN
JANUARY 24 1925

HALLEY'S COMET Visible April 15 to July 1, 1910, and with telescope to the end of the year.

The comet is seen in the morning, April 15 to May 17. It crosses the sun's disc May 18, and is then visible after sunset, being of great size and brilliancy.

May 20, visible for 1 hour after sunset, or until 8.15 P. M.

May 21, visible for 2 hours after sunset, or until 9.20 P. M.

May 23, visible for 3 hours 15 minutes after sunset, or until 10.35 P. M.

May 24, visible for 3 hours 23 minutes after sunset, or until 10.48 P. M.

May 26, visible for 3 hours 50 minutes after sunset, or until 11.15 P. M.

May 27, visible for 4 hours after sunset, or until 11.25 P. M.

May 28, visible for 4 hours 5 minutes after sunset, or until 11.30 P. M.

May 30, visible for 3 hours 50 minutes after sunset, or until 11.15 P. M.

112

422. - CHERBOURG. - Revue du 14 Juillet - Le Préfet Maritime passant en revue les Troupes Coloniales

Collection T. b., Cherbourg

Postcards of all wars starting with the Boer War are collected. French, British and American troops were all painted and photographed during World War I.

fires had razed many other sections of the fast growing cities of the United States.

Each town took great pride in its fire-fighting equipment and the men who used it. In many towns the most exclusive club was the volunteer fire department. This custom of having volunteer fire fighters still exists in many small New England towns. The fire engines were exhibited on parade on special holidays and postcards were made showing the engines on display and at work, putting out local fires. This category of collecting is very rewarding for the diligent deltiologist since there were few towns that did not have their fire-fighting equipment photographed for picture postcards that were sold locally.

Night photography was a difficult if not impossible feat for the rather primitive equipment photographers had to work with at the start of this century. Lightning storms could be rather realistically portrayed by the darkening of a day photograph and the artistic addition of some lightning rays flashing across the sky.

Postcards commemorating or announcing the appearance of Halley's comet in 1910 were made. Edmund Halley had predicted this phenomenon in the eighteenth century and it was anticipated before and discussed long after it had finally appeared on schedule. All predictable natural phenomena were subjects for picture postcards that could be printed and sold well in advance of the event and the total eclipse of the sun on 24 January 1925, was duly recorded for posterity.

If a truly disastrous event of great import had taken place before the postcard photographers could record it, the artist took over from the photographer and reconstructed the horror for postcard collectors. In this manner one could get an idea of how terrible the Chicago fire of 1871 had been even though picture postcards were unheard of at that early date. The San Francisco earthquake and fire were also excellent subjects for disaster-loving collectors.

If an artist or photographer had the opportunity to record a disaster of national or international proportions, his postcards were destined for great success and were assured a large market. However, even small local disasters had sufficient market to justify their being recorded. Long after the disaster occurred, the cards had meaning for those who were there when it happened, and they were purchased for a long period following the event.

113

13

View Cards

Whether one's home is Paris, France; New Orleans, Louisiana; or Devon, England; it's a sure bet that picture postcards printed at the beginning of this century can be found with views of the old hometown as it looked at that time. People tend to be somewhat sentimental about their geographical origins and thousands of today's collectors search for postcards of the one small geographical region that has special meaning for them.

The manner in which these early photographic postcards were made and marketed is rather interesting. One will find, for instance, that the publisher noted on the cards (when he is identified at all) is almost always local and is usually the former proprietor of a variety store, newstand, or in the case of American view cards, the local drugstore. Therefore, there are thousands upon thousands of 'publishers' of cards with local views.

Not only the publisher, but also the photographer was often a local person. Hundreds of photographs of a town's main thoroughfare, public buildings, monuments and historic sites as well as private houses of architectural note were taken. These cards are not only a record of how things looked in the early 1900s, but are usually also examples of the work of the leading photographers of each area.

At the beginning of this century German postcard manufacturers and printers had many agents in various parts of the world who traveled from one town to another picking up or even taking the photographs and taking orders from the local stores that were listed on the cards as 'publishers'. The cards were then printed in Germany and sent or delivered to the publisher. This was an important trade for Germany before World War I and of course was discontinued as soon as hostilities began. American and British postcard firms soon went into business to fill in the gap and cards of hometown views in both countries were printed locally thereafter. Although it was a business that

The beginning of the century was a time when architectural wonders were being built at a rapid rate. All were recorded on picture postcards. Municipal Building, New York.

Although these cards have divided backs they are still multi-view, fashioned after the 'Gruss aus' type of an earlier time.

114

City skylines changed rapidly at beginning of the century. San Francisco was the site of a devastating earthquake in 1906.

A 'Gruss aus' card with artist's rendition of waterfront in Hamburg.

Early view of Pike's Peak by Detroit Publishing Company, 1902.

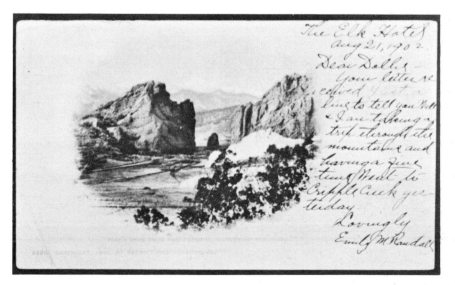

dealt in pennies, any printer could reproduce photographs on postcards and, while in many cases the quality did not compare with the German cards, the sentiment for one's hometown was such that they still sold in quantity.

The earliest of the picture postcards with hometown views or views of vacation spots are multi-view cards patterned after the

PICTURESQUE DEVON.
The Harbour, Lynmouth.

PICTURESQUE DEVON.
Footbridge near Watersmeet, Lynton.

There was no corner of the British Isles that was not recorded by artists and photographers. These two are from a Tuck series of 'Picturesque Devon'.

Scenes of London at turn of century.

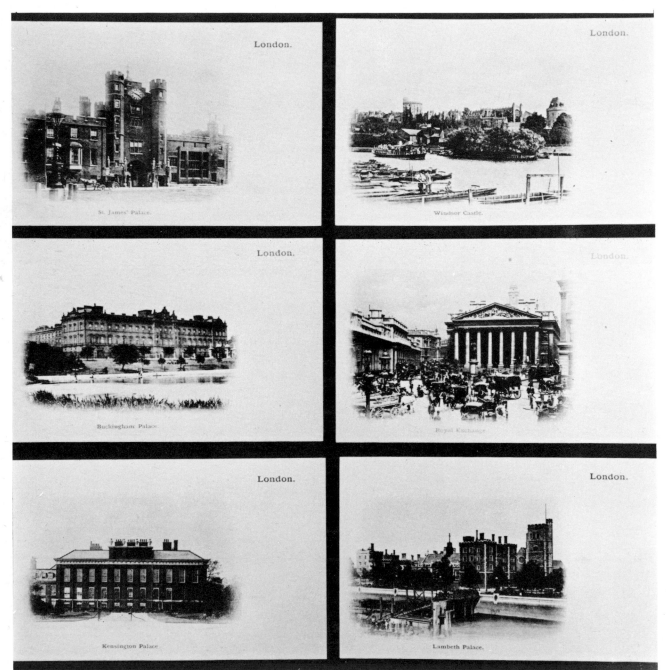

London. St. James' Palace.

London. Windsor Castle.

London. Buckingham Palace.

London. Royal Exchange.

London. Kensington Palace.

London. Lambeth Palace.

Views from almost any spot in the world can be found on old picture postcards.

The Eiffel Tower was photographed from every possible angle. Of special interest is the illustration taken from the top of the tower showing the shadow stretching across the Seine.

'Gruss Aus' cards of Austria and Germany. Vacation areas were photographed from every possible angle and cards printed as souvenirs or for tourists to send home to less fortunate friends and relatives. These are mostly black and white photographic cards, but in many cases the photographs were hand-colored or tinsel-applied.

As buildings are torn down at a rapid rate to make room for more parked cars and housing developments, and highway networks change the entire topography of a city or town, the early photographic postcards of various areas of the world become more than just collectors' items; they are important documentation of how an area looked at the beginning of this century. Nowhere is there a more complete pictorial record of a way of life that has disappeared. Because the cards were mailed everywhere in the world one is just as apt to find a card showing how Paris looked in 1900 in Wisconsin as he is to find a card from Chicago, Illinois, in London. This is what makes the hobby of picture postcard collecting so interesting for those who travel. Foreign view cards are plentiful in America and American views can easily be found in England and on the Continent.

If one were fortunate to have been able to travel at the end of the last century and the beginning of this one, one's friends always expected to be kept in touch by the inexpensive means of picture postcards. Everyone sent them and if he didn't he was considered to have been neglectful of those back home. Usually the postcards went into an album which was proudly shown to visitors. Messages were usually short and simple. 'Father was here today' was written on the back of a postcard with a view of the Panama Canal in the process of being built or on a card that showed a view of Montmartre. 'Leaving today for Geneva' might be found on a postcard showing views of Lucerne.

117

Exotic Japanese postcards show views of city of Osaka surrounded by embossed and gilded designs.

Night views could be further embellished by artists who worked from daytime photographs. Moons, stars and lighted windows were added.

Historical societies and local libraries are beginning to realise more and more the value of old picture postcards of the area in which they are located. Cities and towns that were especially hard hit by bombs during two wars can be visualised as they originally looked from the many picture postcards that can be found today.

A collector who specialises in views of just one town or locality will find post offices, the main business areas (usually including a good shot of the store in which the postcard was originally purchased) early factory buildings and any tourist attractions the town might have had. Although view postcards are still available in most localities, tourists are not apt to send them as readily as they once did. In this age of jet travel and consistently poor mail delivery service the postcards are most often delivered long after the tourist has returned home.

118

14

Of Ladies, Love and Leisure

Picture postcards of the early part of the twentieth century not only give us an idea of what the world looked like at the time, but also a rather clear picture of people, social customs and costume which underwent great changes following Victoria's restrictive reign. We can follow the hand-holding courtship of a couple on postcards evidently taken from drawings that had been used in *Scribner's Magazine* around the beginning of the century. The woman is never without her large ornate picture hat and the couple never seem to progress further than hand-holding during the courtship.

Female models in large picture hats, popular at the turn of the century, were the subject of many brightly colored picture postcards. The artist, Philip Boileau, was noted for his winsome, demure ladies in large fashionable headgear. Courtship and marriage were treated mainly in traditional Victorian fashion on the earlier cards and the man and woman are seldom touching. As the twentieth century moved on a bit, women's clothing became less constrictive and the postcard subjects became somewhat less restricted if they portrayed couples in love. Captions became more suggestive and couples not only held hands but they kissed and 'spooned' on the parlor sofa. Suggestive 'tunnel of love' scenes as well as photographs or drawings of couples in isolated places flirting or kissing were thought to be somewhat daring for the time. Many actors and actresses found needed work posing for these photographs.

Two postcards that were popular charted the 'Course of Romance' on a mythological map of 'Truelove River' or 'Betrothal Bay'. These cards were considered extremely clever at the time of their publication and illustrate all of the problems lovers had to go through to reach the point of marriage. Postcards with lovers were popular in every country and they can be found with the captions translated into many languages. Those that were slightly titillating were also collected and one theme that is seen over and over is the intrusion of a third person such as a bellboy or golf caddy on a married couple about to 'spoon'. However, on many of the postcards of this type the only 'intruder' is the viewer of the card.

Women's skirts were still long at the turn of the century and figures were molded with the assistance of heavy corsets and stays. Any postcard showing a woman's legs (usually only from the knees down) was considered to be daring. Nudes were acceptable only if the picture was a reproduction of a famous painting or sculpture. One didn't embarrass the recipient of a postcard by

119

sending anything more suggestive through the mail. There is little doubt that pornographic cards were made in quantity, but these were not sent through the mail unless they were concealed in envelopes. They were not collected in quantity by the thousands of collectors who looked for novelty and beauty rather than vicarious thrills for their albums. Because of their rarity, pornographic or even suggestive picture postcards are among the most expensive for collectors who are determined to add such cards to their albums or files.

One can still find a rather complete history of the theater of England and America of the period leading up to World War I on picture postcards. Among the most popular are full cast photographs of plays that were especially popular. Revered stage stars, opera singers and ballet artists were all photographed in the costumes of their more successful roles and many stagestruck collectors filled albums with their portraits. 'Life upon the wicked stage' was another popular theme of the period and many postcards depicting the dangers of 'stage life' were published. Opera

120

Gruss aus München.

"Grinning like a Cheshire Cat."

"I didn't know that Cheshire cats always grinned ; in fact, I didn't know that Cheshire cats could grin."

"They all can," said the Duchess, "and most of 'em do."

"I don't know of any that do," said Alice.

"You don't know much" said the Duchess, "and that's a fact."
— Alice in Wonderland.

Oh that funny feeling!

A Happy New Year.

The Result! A happy New Year.

Tired nature's sweet restorer, balmy sleep.

HANDS ACROSS THE SEA

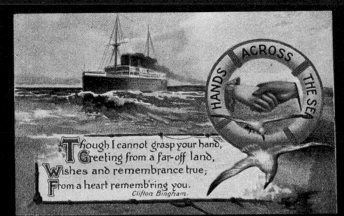

Though I cannot grasp your hand,
Greeting from a far-off land,
Wishes and remembrance true;
From a heart remembring you.
Clifton Bingham.

HANDS ACROSS THE SEA

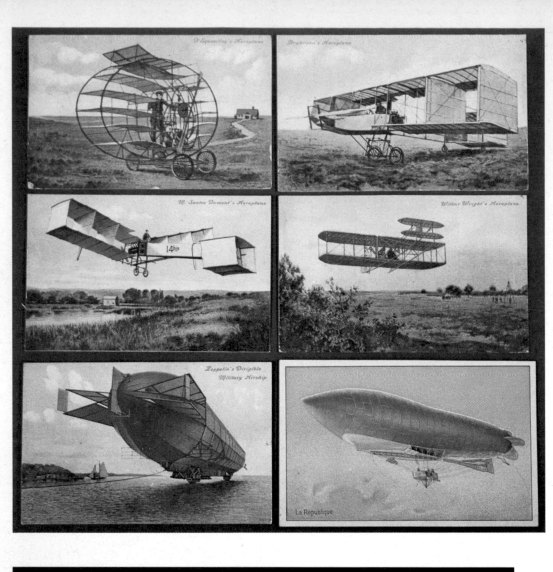

D'Equevilley's Aeroplane. Brabazon's Aeroplane. M. Santos Dumont's Aeroplane. Wilbur Wright's Aeroplane. Zeppelin's Dirigible Military Airship. La Republique.

We have a lovely lamp in our drawing-room, you can turn it so low that you can scarcely see at all.

STATE OF WISCONSIN. STATE OF CONNECTICUT. STATE OF VERMONT. STATE OF NEW YORK. STATE OF MISSOURI. State of Massachusetts.

Top left. All early flying machines, from balloons to dirigibles, are sought by collectors today.

Top right. Two romantic postcards: the lower one shows the use of electric light for romantic setting.

Bottom. Pretty girls were designed to represent the states on this set.

YESTERDAY!

MY CHAUFFEUR...

FOREVER.

TOMORROW...

OUT FOR FUN.

TO-DAY?

Philip Boileau was an artist who specialized in painting beautiful women.

and ballet were considered socially acceptable, but the legitimate theater had a long way to go before society would accept its actors as artists.

Postcards were adapted from posters to advertise stage extravaganzas and the new motion pictures did not miss the opportunity to advertise their latest productions and their most popular stars. In this brand new and miraculous art form, where photography was the medium, the still pictures of the glamorous movie stars went a long way to publicise both the stars and their pictures. Movie historians can still find a great deal of information about the early years of the art on these publicity postcards, many of which were issued by the studios in Hollywood.

The interiors of theaters, especially opera houses, were extremely popular subjects. So many of these elaborate nineteenth century buildings have been torn down or remodeled that the postcards are sometimes the only record we have that they existed at all.

There is some difference between American and British picture

Well my dear and where have I seen you before?

Beauty is a good letter of introduction.
But you *know* me!

Flirtations and kissing were depicted on photographic posed cards.

Why don't you marry the girl.

IN THE TUNNEL.

Thousands of actors and actresses found work posing for postcard pictures such as those seen here.

Copyright, 1907, by I. & M. O.   19

A DUET.

Copyright, 1907, by I. & M. O.   8

A TEA SPOON.

Opposite: cast photographs of popular plays, vaudeville and musical shows.

124

Below and right: 'Chart of Betrothal Bay' was clever postcard; that on the right is of 'hands across the sea' variety.

postcards that represented college life at the beginning of this century. American colleges appear to be places where the only subject taught was football while some serious postcards showing the conferring of degrees at Oxford and other serious subjects having to do with university life in Great Britain can be found. However, the British universities were not without their

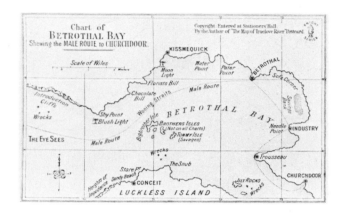

125

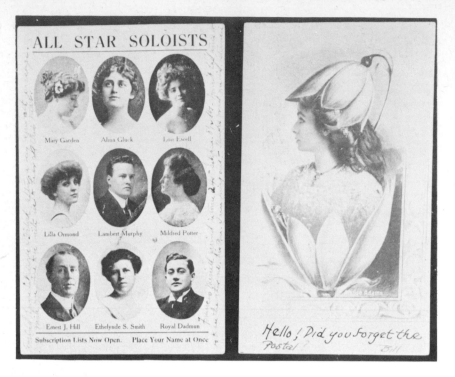

Postcard probably adapted from poster painted in style of Delft tiles advertises 'new moving pictures'.

humorous cards and one especially popular series, entitled 'Americans at Oxford', managed to poke fun at the ignorance of young American ladies who obviously were visiting that venerable campus unchaperoned. For instance, one card in this series shows two attractive young American women coming through the door of what appears to be students' apartments and the caption: American ladies (bursting into an undergraduate's room) 'Beg pardon, young men, we had no idea these ancient ruins were inhabited!'

Popular sports and the players were depicted on many picture postcards. College football in the United States had evolved from a combination of the British sports, rugby and soccer, and the first intercollegiate football conference had been formed by Harvard, Princeton, Yale, Rutgers and Columbia in 1876. Professional football was first played at Latrobe, Pennsylvania, in 1895, but it was the college teams that were the subject of many souvenir picture postcards.

The football cards were published for every major college team in the country and often the pictures included pennants of the school being waved by wholesome pretty girls, none of whom would have been admitted as students at the time. One Tuck 'oilette' series of American football included all of the important

Top left: musicians and actors were all well known since there were many theaters and traveling troups during the early part of this century; postcard on right of Maude Adams is especially charming.
Above (left and right): 'Stage Life' series showed the theater as being no place for a 'good girl'.

Opposite.
1st row: Hollywood stars were shown in costume of their most popular roles.
2nd row: group of Oxford University postcards from beginning of this century.
3rd row: 'Americans at Oxford' series pokes fun at ignorance of American ladies on subject of school architecture and traditions.

126

VIOLA DANA
As Ardita Far... am in "The Off-Shore Pirate"
A Metro Production

ALICE TERRY
As Princess Flavia in "The Prisoner of Zenda"
A Metro-Rex Ingram Production

MARY MILES MINTER
As Rosalie Beck with in "The Heart Specialist"
A Realart Picture

MAY MORNING ON MAGDALEN TOWER

Drawn by Sydney P. Hall, M.V.O.]   ["Graphic" Copyright.
THE CONFERRING OF DEGREES AT OXFORD.

ARMS OF SCHOOLS

AMERICANS IN OXFORD.

AMERICANS IN OXFORD.

AMERICANS IN OXFORD.

127

RAY – RAY – RAY –
WIL-YUMS-YAMS-YUMS!
WIL – YUMS !

college teams with the most popular cheer printed at the bottom of the card for anyone who was inclined to memorise the inane verse for the big game of the season. The Tuck cards also included the college seal. Artist-drawn pictures of members of college football teams depicted the players as strong, handsome and muscular and helped to create the image of the American athletic hero of the period. College players for the leading football teams often were known for their brain as well as their brawn in those early days and were revered by young women as heroes.

Other national and international sporting events were documented on picture postcards. The British sports of rugby and cricket were portrayed on serious and comic cards. Among the most charming is a series by artist E. P. Kinsella who devised a small, bright-eyed urchin playing cricket.

Crew, hockey, mountain climbing, skiing, skating, toboganning and even bullfighting were not neglected by the postcard designers and publishers. These were sold in whatever country the particular sport was popular. Feats of strength and endurance that took place during the first fifteen or twenty years of this century were documented on postcards and collected for albums.

American baseball players and teams of the first half of this century are well-documented on great numbers of cards that were given away in chewing gum and cigarette packages. However, picture postcards of an earlier date record the great stadiums that were built to house the various teams of the American national sport. Not only national teams, but local teams that were the pride of their home towns, were duly photographed and postcards made. The American game of baseball that descended from the British games of rounders and cricket really came into its own following the Civil War and by 1900 teams were well established in almost every town in the United States.

From the foregoing it should be obvious that few leisure activities escaped the brush, pen or camera of the picture postcard designer. One could purchase postcards showing humans engaged in almost any activity. Once again, there are collectors who specialise in postcards of any category of sports, pictures of pretty girls, couples 'spooning' or special colleges or college teams. It might be worthwhile for collectors to remember that not only a few, but millions of postcards were once available that illustrated all of these forms of human activity. The 'line-ups' of many of the local teams to be found on baseball, cricket, football and other athletic team cards often contain grandfathers of people we know.

Above left: large stadiums were built in which were played the American national sport.
Above right: pretty girls were shown cheering their favorite teams; cheers were printed for anyone who wanted to join in.
Above: photographs were taken of every feat of daring, including the conquering of mountain summits by men.

128

15
American Patriotic Postcards

Huld issued this set of instalment cards of American 'Uncle Sam'.

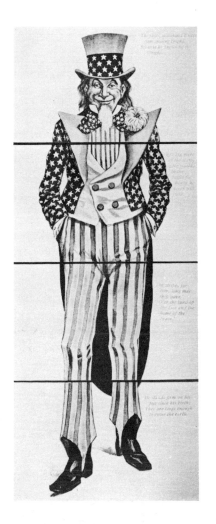

At the beginning of this century the American market for picture postcards of a patriotic nature was quickly assessed by British and German manufacturers and a great many cards were printed in those countries for sale to Americans overseas. Some rather lovely and interesting series were made by Tuck and were probably never seen by the avid British collectors. Tuck issued series of 'American Presidents' and 'Homes of the Presidents'. Both of these were very popular and many albums with the entire series have been found in the United States by the new wave of collectors.

By the turn of the century the western part of the United States was being documented by artists in that country, but Raphael Tuck & Sons had its own artist, Harry Payne, paint scenes showing the settlers on horseback. It is not known whether he did these from photographs, life, or imagination. American postcard manufacturers also recognised the value of colorful American Indians in full feathered regalia as subjects, and in many cases these early portraits are the only ones existing of the tribal leaders of the American Indians. Both paintings and photographs of Indians were made as card subjects. Tuck also printed portraits of some of the Indian chiefs.

American patriotism also provided an extra bonanza for postcard manufacturers in the field of greeting cards. National holidays such as Washington's and Lincoln's birthdays, Independence Day (the 4th of July), Memorial Day, and Thanksgiving were all indigenous to the United States and manufacturers abroad answered the need for postcards to be sent out on all those holidays.

More interesting to American historian-collectors than the greeting cards made for national holidays and the series made to appeal to American patriotic sentiments, are the cards made for presidential campaigns. The postcard was discovered to be a cheap and effective means of communicating party preferences during the few elections held during the postcard collecting craze and many candidates took advantage of this fact. One particularly interesting card of this period is that sent out by that three-time loser for the presidency, William Jennings Bryan, in 1908. The card, which is a three-fold die-cut issue, attempts to prove that Bryan is a 'dead ringer' for George Washington. When folded, the card shows two portraits, side-by-side, of George

129

Top: American holidays such as Independence Day, Washington's Birthday and Memorial Day were the cause for sending patriotic postcards.
Above – left and center: Lincoln's Birthday postcards are sought by collectors who specialize in 'Lincoln' examples.
Right: rare card showing 'Uncle Sam' endorsing Theodore Roosevelt for President.

Far left: new woman voter and portrait of William Howard Taft, 'our new President'.
Left: World War I postcard with portrait of President Wilson.

Building decorated in bunting for impending visit of William Howard Taft.

Die-cut campaign card for three-time presidential loser William Jennings Bryan.

Washington taken from the famous portrait of the first President of the United States by Gilbert Stuart. Washington's signature appears beneath the twin portraits. The mailing or address side of the card has a portrait of Bryan and the same portrait of Washington in the upper right-hand corner with the patriotic symbols of the flag, the eagle and the capitol building. However, if one lifts the flap on the left 'Washington's' hair and eighteenth century dress come off and the face is revealed to be that of William Jennings Bryan in contemporary dress and without Washington's white wig. One can immediately deduce that Bryan and Washington look absolutely alike and therefore, one is supposed to assume that Bryan is the same sort of presidential material as Washington. The card couldn't have made any important impact on American voters who rejected Bryan for the third and last time. The portraits of Bryan and Washington are, of course, cleverly doctored to create the 'remarkable resemblance'.

American collectors of today specialise in several types of patriotic postcards. Most especially, they search for cards with portraits of George Washington and Abraham Lincoln. Many of these were published by American companies and still more were published, or at least printed, abroad. Since neither the Washington nor Lincoln issues reflect history contemporary with postcard

131

publishing, except as these cards were printed to commemorate certain anniversaries of the death, birth or terms of office of either one, it is surprising that the cards with portraits of both of these great Americans are so popular with American collectors except that they appeal to their patriotism.

A presidential postcard that is more reflective of the first period of postcard collecting and shows American Presidents in a light more contemporary with the great period of postcard manufacture, is the '25 Presidents' card copyright by the P.L. Novelty Co. in New York in 1901 and printed in Germany. It has framed engravings of all the Presidents up to and including Theodore Roosevelt. In 1909 the same card was printed by the Finn Press of New York with the addition of President William Howard Taft. Political campaign cards showing portraits of the Presidents who ran for office during the first nineteen years of this century should be carefully preserved as pictorial records of American political history.

Another historical postcard that is sought by American collectors is that made to commemorate Theodore Roosevelt's American Fleet 'Peace Voyage' in 1909. Roosevelt sent twenty ships on a 42,227 mile voyage around the world and the return of the fleet was the occasion for printing a celebration issue that was copyrighted by H. T. Cook of New York.

Events of a patriotic or political nature represented by postcards of the period preceding World War I are sought by many collectors. The building of the Panama Canal, begun during Theodore Roosevelt's administration and completed during Wilson's, was a popular subject. Theodore Roosevelt's political campaigns were commemorated in the publication of portrait postcards and the Teddy Bear, popular as a symbol of the Roosevelt administration, was a favorite subject for picture postcards that were sent to children.

Postcard collectors' clubs have lately become popular once again in the United States and many collectors search for examples of a historical nature representing their particular geographical areas. President's homes and libraries, once neglected, are now being restored and all of the buildings associated with American history that were once recorded on picture postcards have come to have more meaning than they once did. Anniversaries of historical events were represented by postcards and these are also being preserved.

On the whole, however, Americans are not as chauvinistic as one might imagine when it comes to collecting and are just as apt to desire a complete set of Tuck's 'British Royalty' as they are a set of 'American Presidents'.

Postcards for Rally Day, which is no longer celebrated.

132

16

British Patriotic Postcards

During the period when picture postcards first became popular, Queen Victoria was in her dotage and manufacturers looked for any excuse to tie the craze for collecting to her Majesty by making claims that the Queen did, indeed, collect albums full of picture postcards. In this manner the British publishers hoped to give the hobby at least unofficial endorsement of Royal patronage. There seems to be no evidence that Victoria, incurable collector of many other objects, gave album space to the little colorful cards that had become such an important part of everyone's daily mail. However, this did not deter manufacturers from using royalty as subjects of their cards.

The history of the popularity of picture postcard collecting in Great Britain coincides almost totally with the Edwardian period. Edward VII's reign, between the years 1901 and 1910, is rather completely documented on picture postcards. Portraits of many of the King's relatives as well as events of the decade are all colorfully recorded for us and there is, perhaps, no better social, political, scientific or artistic documentation of the Edwardian period than that to be found on an assortment of British picture postcards. Reigning monarchs of England have been fair game as subjects of picture postcards since Edward's time, but the collecting hobby that achieved such immense popularity in England during Edward's reign began to wane following his death and we look to other media now, especially film, for the documentation of the lives of later members of the royal family.

If one is collecting postcards related to the coronation of Edward VII, the earliest one to search for would be a Tuck card printed with a message from the King to his people explaining his illness and inability to attend the coronation on the date that was first set aside for that event. This message had a strong impact on a people that had loved their venerable Queen and were, perhaps, somewhat apprehensive in welcoming to the throne her sixty-year-old son who had been forbidden by his mother to take part in the affairs of state while she lived.

In his message the King told his countrymen, 'On the eve of my Coronation, an event which I look upon as one of the most solemn and important in my life, I am anxious to express to my people at home and in the Colonies and in India my heartfelt appreciation of the deep sympathy which they have manifested towards me during the time that my life was in such imminent danger.

'The postponement of the ceremony owing to illness caused, I fear, much inconvenience and trouble to all those who intended

133

H. R. H. THE PRINCESS OF WALES

H. R. H. THE PRINCE OF WALES

"GOD BLESS THE PRINCE OF WALES"

GOD BLESS THE PRINCE OF WALES

134

Souvenir 'song' postcard of coronation of George V.

The fairy-tale coronation coach used once again in 1937.

Opposite.
1st row: (left) postcard relating to the coronation of Edward VII: (center and right) portraits of the Prince and Princess of Wales – 'Photochromes' by Tuck.
2nd row: (left and center) coronation souvenir cards from the coronation of His Majesty, George V; (right) coronation scene from 1911.
3rd row: the Prince of Wales was well-known and liked all over the world before he became ruler for a brief period.

to celebrate it, but their disappointment was borne by them with admirable patience and temper. The prayers of my people for recovery were heard, and I now offer up my deepest gratitude to Divine Providence for having preserved my life and given me strength to fulfill the important duties which devolve upon me as the Sovereign of this great Empire.'

The message, circulated on thousands of Tuck postcards, was dated 8 August 1902. Of course, the coronation did take place and many souvenir postcards were issued in commemoration of the event as they have been for subsequent coronations and every event having to do with the royal family since Edward's reign. Coronation souvenirs have a special place, even in modern albums, but those with scenes or symbols of Edward's coronation and portraits of his wife, the Princess Alexandra of Denmark, are highly prized by collectors everywhere since they also represent the age when postcards were considered an important popular art form, and the history of the Edwardian age represents for collectors the golden age of design and manufacture.

Following Edward's death, and one can be assured that the funeral ceremonies were duly recorded on picture postcards, the coronation and reign of George V were recorded for the postcard collectors. However, World War I interrupted the interest in

135

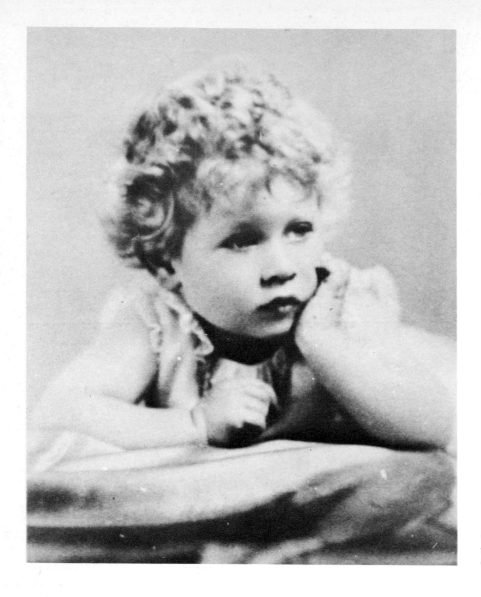

Child portrait on postcard of the present Queen of England, Queen Elizabeth II.

collecting and the manufacture of cards was all but suspended. Royalty is never neglected by manufacturers of souvenir items and postcards representing George V's reign can be found. After George's death in 1936, Edward VIII's short reign was also recorded. The popular Prince of Wales (the late Duke of Windsor) had seldom been out of the limelight during his youth and all through his boyhood the postcard printers had issued cards showing portraits of him at various stages of his development. He had taken many official tours at home and abroad and was immensely popular throughout the world by the time he was made King of England. His reign, of course, was cut short when he abdicated the throne to marry the American divorcée, Mrs Simpson. That occasion was more a subject for the tabloids than the postcard designers.

Picture postcards of George VI and his attractive family were issued in smaller numbers because of World War II. Previous to World War II, his two young daughters sat to photographers and artists with some frequency, and many of these portraits were then printed on picture postcards.

As souvenirs of royal events, picture postcards give us the most complete record of what actually took place and how the country and the principals in those events looked at the time. However, there is little doubt that the period during the reign of Edward VII, when postcards were most popular, is the period of British royal history that is most completely documented.

136

17

Coins and Stamps on Postcards

Deltiology is a hobby that is, of course, closely related to philately. There are postcards that are also directly related to the hobby of numismatology. Collectors in both of these related fields are aware of the many postcards that were printed and embossed with coins and stamps of many countries. Ottmar Zieher of Munich printed series of 'stamp' cards by grouping the stamps of each nation around the national symbol or shield, leaving a small space for the message. These stamps are printed in true colors and are remarkably accurate in every detail. There are now many collectors who specialise in Ottmar Zieher stamp cards and auction prices for these cards have been rising steadily for the past few years.

Zieher also made many 'coin' cards with national flags arranged across the tops of the cards along with the coins of that

Ottmar Zieher stamp cards are realistic and colorful and in high demand by both postcard and stamp collectors.

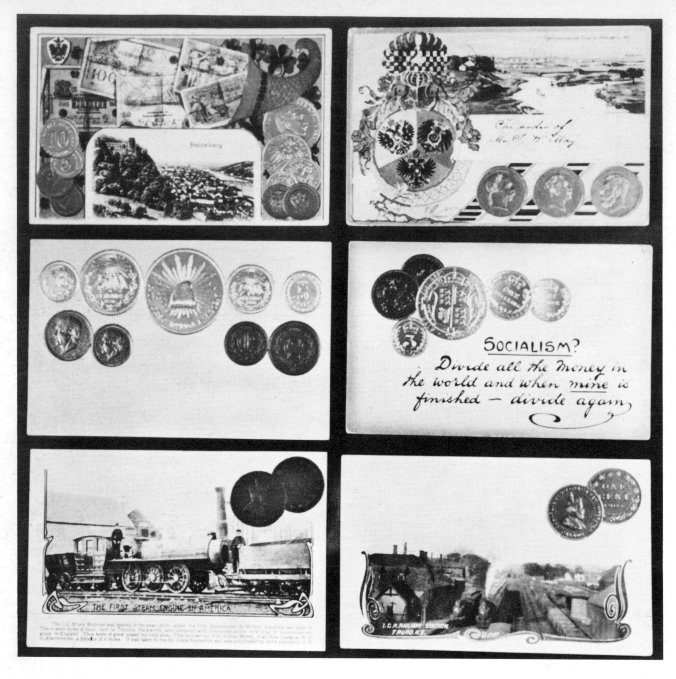

particular nation. The usefulness of these cards to travelers on the 'grand tour' was increased by Zieher placing the rates of exchange for the coins of each country on his cards.

The Zieher cards are spectacularly printed and the embossments are so real that one might expect to be able to pick the coins off the cards and spend them. Great care was taken to represent the exact metallic colors in each embossed coin. Thus, gold, copper and silver colors are all represented on one card and each coin is designated by denomination to simplify identification and comparative values.

The production of stamp and coin cards was prohibited in England and these cards could not be sent through the mail in that country. However, continental rules were somewhat more relaxed and Ottmar Zieher and several other publishers were very successful in marketing their stamp and coin cards elsewhere. Many of them were purchased, not for mailing, but as welcome additions to collectors' albums. All Zieher cards are numbered and represent coins of just about every nation that had its own currency previous to World War I: Latin American nations and all European countries were included.

Coins, bank notes and stamps were all portrayed realistically on this group.

Top right: flags of all nations held by beautiful girls couldn't miss as album postcards. Right: group of postcards with portraits of ladies all with applied real hair. Far right: real feathers were glued on these cards to add realism.

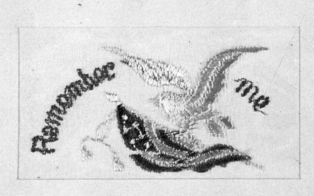

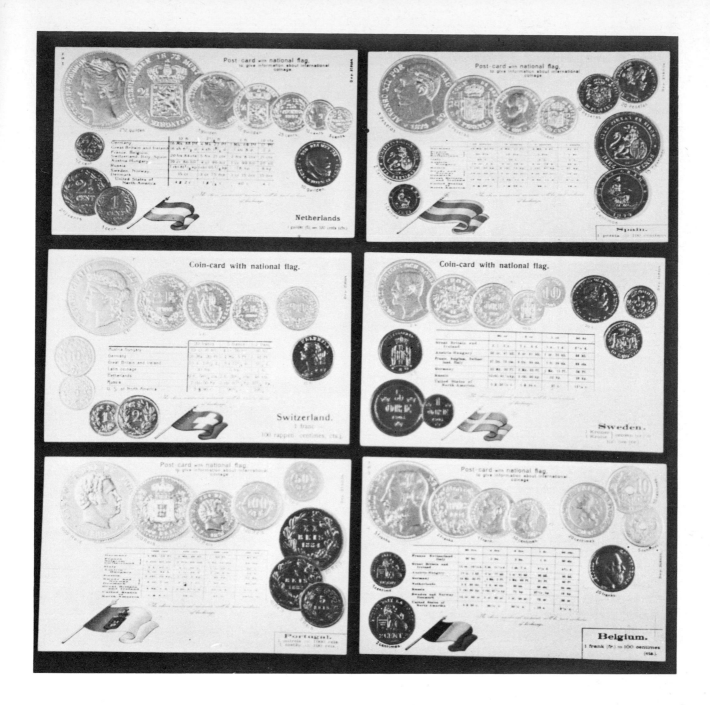

Ottmar Zieher coin cards were a convenience for travelers.

View cards with an embossed Canadian penny were issued and there are two of these illustrated here, one of the 'first steam engine in America', and the other a view of the railway station in Truro, Nova Scotia. Coin cards with bank notes and views of continental subjects were also printed on cards with divided backs. An interesting propaganda card (page 138) has the message, 'SOCIALISM? Divide all the money in the world and when *mine* is finished . . . Divide again'. The coins are British.

An interesting group of bank check cards were printed as greeting cards. The sender could fill in the signature and the 'check' would bring greetings to the recipient of '365 happy days' or 'ten thousand joys' for the New Year.

An unusual primitive type of card was made with the use of cancelled postage stamps. The stamps were cut and used as a material for a form of decoupage card with simple hand-drawn or hand-painted backgrounds to complete the designs. Round stamps were used as spinning wheels. Other stamps with portraits such as Washington or Lincoln were trimmed and used

Top: group of hand-embroidered silk cards made during and after World War I in France and Belgium. Bottom: two cards made of bamboo.

141

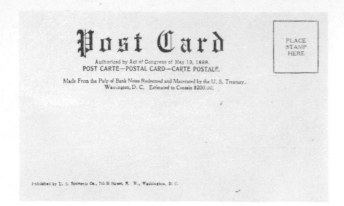

as pictures on the wall, another dimension being added by the drawing of a few lines to depict a string holder and a nail. Particularly imaginative are stamps cut to resemble prints of 'fabric' for kimonos on Japanese figures. The cutting and pasting on these cards, as well as the simple art work, required a certain amount of talent and feeling for design. Of rather special interest is the card illustrated with stamps cut to the shape of sailboats and heavily cancelled stamps cut to resemble rocks in the foreground.

While these novelty one-of-a-kind handmade stamp cards have enormous appeal for some, it is the Ottmar Zieher stamp and coin cards that are most sought by deltiologists. These specialist collectors are all aware of the amount of cards in each numbered series and will go to great lengths and expense to fill in their collections.

One other postcard type that has to do with the application of money to its manufacture is illustrated here. It was published by the U.S. Souvenir Company of Washington, D.C. and was sold as a souvenir of that city. As designated on the card it was 'made from the pulp of bank notes redeemed and macerated by the U.S. Treasury, Washington, D.C.' and 'estimated to contain $200.00'. On the picture side of the card is an engraving of the 'treasury building where this macerated money is made'. This practice was discontinued and the cards are rarely found today.

One has only to handle an Ottmar Zieher coin or stamp card to become convinced that the superior color printing and embossing methods used by that company to reproduce so faithfully the coins and stamps of many nations is a lost art. These cards that once cost a few pennies would now be prohibitively expensive to reproduce. Collectors, in their zeal to own complete sets of Ottmar Zieher coin and stamp cards, are well aware of this.

Top: postcard made from 'macerated money' by the U.S. Souvenir Company. Bottom: postcards with fake checks were issued for Christmas and New Year's greetings.

142

18
Novelty Postcards

One of the most fascinating categories of picture postcard collecting is the gathering of the wide variety of novelty cards that were made. A great many different types can be placed in this convenient category. Some of the cards are extremely rare today owing to the fact that many were made with the addition of fragile material, and others were manufactured as jigsaw puzzle cards that had to be broken up or cut in order to be put back together again – few have survived. The same is true of paper doll postcards and other cut-outs that were made mostly to be sent to children.

Into the category of novelty cards can be placed those that had appliqués or additions of material added to the basic postcard. Pictures of ladies had real hair glued on or hats made of a variety of materials pasted on the heads. Real cloth dresses were pasted on children or ladies and these constitute another group of 'add-on' cards. Cards with bits of lace, fur and real ribbon also are included in this category.

A great many cards with birds as subjects were made with real feathers from each bird glued onto the bodies. Some effort was made by the manufacturers and artists to have the species of birds look as real as possible. Of special beauty are the peacocks with real iridescent peacock feathers adorning the tails.

Another method of adorning postcards with extra realistic material are the animal cards in which the shape of the animal is cut out of a fur-like fabric and pasted on the printed card. Tiny felt pennants with the name of a town or school printed on them were pasted to stock cards, thus making the cards 'to order' for the area or place where they were to be sold.

Miniature calendars were also pasted on stock cards, thereby enabling the manufacturer to use the same postcard plate year after year. The little calendars could be removed and kept in a pocket or purse for easy referral throughout the year.

During a period when handwork was cheaply done by underpaid women and children it was a small matter to paste bits of cloth, tinsel, beading, fur, lace, feathers, ribbon or other materials on cards that could still be sold for a few cents. Most of these appliqué cards were made in Germany prior to World War I and found a ready international market.

Tiny booklets that included a poem or appropriate quotation for a special holiday were pasted onto elaborately embossed postcards. John Winsch made many of this type and a particularly nice one, a Thanksgiving Day greeting, consists of a colorful embossed cover that opens to include two pages with designs and

143

a quotation from Whittiker printed in gold. The booklet is further bedecked with a green ribbon and under the booklet, the card, itself, shows a painting of two pilgrims sitting at table with a large turkey and very visible aroma (outlined in gold) wafting out the open window while grace is being said. This card is dated 1913 and was obviously delivered by hand or mailed in an envelope since there is a rather sentimental message written on the reverse, but no signs of stamp or cancellation.

Other cards were decorated with tinsel, small transparent beads or finely ground glitter. They were made commercially, but many of the most fascinating tinsel cards were those that were printed with an embossed flower or other colorful printed decoration and a message, initial or name written in glue by the sender. The tinsel was shaken over the glue and the residue blown away. In this manner a card could be attractively personalised for the recipient. Do-it-yourself kits were sold for this purpose and were undoubtedly very popular. White iridescent sparkle was glued to printed winter snow scenes and these were thought to make very

Thanksgiving greeting card published by Winsch around 1913. Beribboned applied booklet has a poem by Whittiker printed in gold and a picture inside of two pilgrims.

144

Postcards made from unusual materials. Top left: birchbark; top right: bamboo wood. Center left: leather; center right: celluloid. Bottom left: peat moss paper; bottom right: wood.

realistic and beautiful Christmas and New Year cards.

Other materials that were added on to picture postcards, usually, but not always, of the greeting card variety, were metal, usually gold color, velvet, real dried flowers or grasses, thinly cut mother-of-pearl or reasonable facsimiles, foil paper, ribbons, etc. Satin material was used on some cards with stuffing to form tiny pin cushions, often heart or flower shaped.

On some cards an entire covering of cloth was applied and the picture or greeting was printed over that. These faced cards eventually gave way to the invention of a kind of paper that resembled satin or faille cloth and was cheaper and easier for the manufacturer.

One interesting kind of appliqué card is the previously mentioned stamp cut-out. Postage stamps of various colors were cut out in various shapes and pasted onto a blank card. The stamps were ingeniously used in the design and often a slight bit of artwork by the maker would add to the realism of the picture. Therefore, an oval cut-out of George Washington's face could be

145

'framed' by the addition of a few inked lines and given further realism by the addition of a 'wire' and 'picture hook'. These cards and their designs have been discussed in the chapter on stamp and coin cards and they are a form of hand-made decoupage cards

Top: by revolving discs in these cards the faces change. Bottom: by working this puzzle card all eleven holes are supposed to show black faces.

146

March 18, 1931

A hold-to-light card showing a faked night scene.

that seemed to be popular for only a short period of time. They can be considered an interesting form of primitive, or hand-made postcard.

Another type of postcard in the add-on category is the mirror card. A tiny mirror was inserted in the card and the message usually told the viewer to look into the glass to see himself. In another of the add-on variety, the recipient didn't have to go to this trouble to view himself since the sender purchased photo insert cards and took the trouble to paste a photograph of himself or the recipient in the space provided.

While cloth seems to have been the most popular material used as add-on interest for picture postcards there is one particularly interesting kind of card using satin patches that is highly collectible and difficult to find today. This is the 'Fab patchwork card' made by M. W. Sharp of Bradford, England. On the face of these cards was pasted a specially woven satin cloth patch with a color printed design. The small ($3\frac{2}{3}$ inches) square patch was to be taken off and sewn together with other like patches made in various series such as 'Arms & Clans', 'Views', 'Flowers and Flags', and 'Portraits of Noted Persons'. The object was to make larger units of the satin pictures.

The side panels of the 'Fab' cards had printed and illustrated directions on how to use the silk patches. The upper corners on some of the cards have the words, 'The Patent Fab Patchwork Card' and 'The Art Needlework Series'. Some of the cards have pictures of a woman sewing the patches together; others have directions such as, 'To Detach satin square cut along dotted line', and the advice, 'Can be worked into artistic cushions, Duchess covers, tea cosies, pin cushions, etc., etc.'

While the Fab cards had patches of printed cloth, there were many others with added cloth panels that were embroidered,

147

Installment cards were novelty for children who received them at holiday time.

148

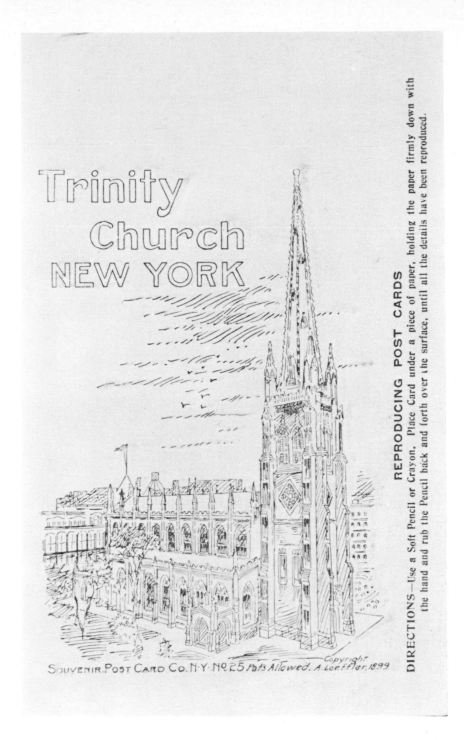

Trinity
Church
NEW YORK

SOUVENIR POST CARD CO. N·Y· No.25 Pat's Allowed. A Loeffler. 1899. Copyright

REPRODUCING POST CARDS

DIRECTIONS—Use a Soft Pencil or Crayon. Place Card under a piece of paper, holding the paper firmly down with the hand and rub the Pencil back and forth over the surface, until all the details have been reproduced.

'Reproducing postcard' copyrighted in 1899: directions for using are on side.

some by machine in a variety of subjects and methods and others by hand. Even more highly prized are the woven silk cards made by T. Stevens in England. The Jacquard loom had been invented in France in 1801 and permitted the weaving of patterns into ribbons. The French had a reputation for making beautiful ribbon that was desired by women all over the world. British manufacturers of ribbon were protected by a tariff on the import of the product so that a prosperous industry in ribbon manufacture had been developed in Coventry through the first half of the nineteenth century. When the tariff was lifted in 1860 it threatened to put the British manufacturers out of business. Thomas Stevens was one of the ribbon makers that almost lost his business due to this situation, but he saved it by experimenting with weaving pictures into his ribbons on looms that were patterned after the French Jacquard looms.

Stevens used a variety of colors and wove ribbons with scenes

149

MUCHEE GOOD LUCK

Suppose-

you hurry

and come home

MASON

IN FOR LIFE

ELK

FATHER CALLS HIM WILLIAM, THE GIRLS ALL CALL HIM WILLIE, MOTHER CALLS HIM WILL, BUT AN ELK SAYS "HELLO BILL"

150

Far left: racial minority groups suffered from being caricatured; on this card a hole is cut where the nose is supposed to be and one puts his thumb through the hole to complete the 'picture'. **Left:** an example of a 'suppose' postcard.

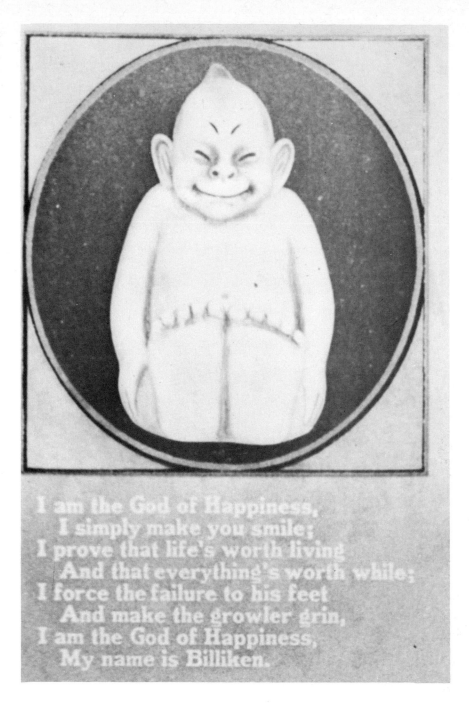

I am the God of Happiness,
I simply make you smile;
I prove that life's worth living
And that everything's worth while;
I force the failure to his feet
And make the growler grin,
I am the God of Happiness,
My name is Billiken.

The 'Billiken' was cartoon character invented for postcards.

Two of series of fraternal organization.

into bookmarks about $1\frac{1}{4}$ inches in width and 6 inches long. His early production, from about 1862–77, consisted almost entirely of bookmarks. In later years Stevens manufactured larger woven pictures that were given as prizes, gifts and souvenirs. Many were made for advertising purposes. Others were incorporated into postcards that are extremely desirable to today's collectors.

Stevensgraphs, most particularly the early bookmarks, have been collected for many years. Many of those made for advertising purposes were for the American as well as the British market. The designs for greeting cards were made and sold over a long period of time since once the looms were set up, a complicated and expensive process, it was necessary to produce a great many of one design in order for it to be profitable.

Thomas Stevens exhibited in the American Centennial Exhibition in Philadelphia in 1876 and sent looms for the exhibit on which were woven commemorative ribbons which were then sold as souvenirs. In the beginning of the twentieth century, during

151

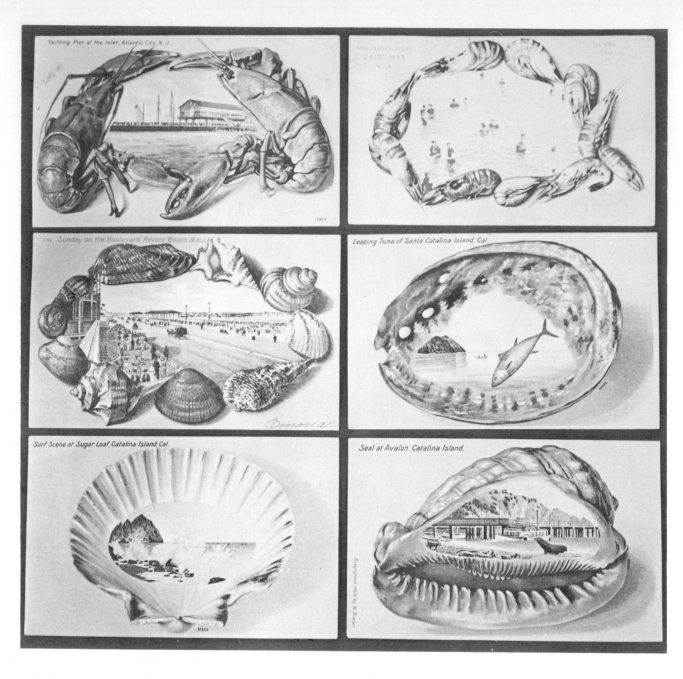

Yachting Pier at the Inlet, Atlantic City, N.J.

Greetings from CAPE MAY N.J. In the surf

Sunday on the Boulevard, Revere Beach, Mass.

Leaping Tuna of Santa Catalina Island, Cal.

Surf Scene at Sugar Loaf, Catalina Island, Cal.

Seal at Avalon, Catalina Island.

the height of the postcard craze, Stevens wove miniature pictures of ships that were inserted in embossed postcard-size mounts. The silk pictures of Thomas Stevens, although manufactured by the millions, are difficult to find today and are highly prized by all postcard collectors. Stevens postcards date from around 1902–20 and the subjects of many of the later wartime cards were ships of the Royal Navy and 'Hands Across the Sea'.

Silk woven cards were made by other manufacturers as well, notably Grant, who also had a factory in Coventry. There is a much wider variety of subject matter in the Grant cards, ranging about a hundred in number. Alpha cards, evidently made by the Stevens Company, were distributed in London by the Messrs. Steibel who owned that trademark. Most of the Alpha cards were greeting cards and the silk patches, unlike the Stevens-labeled cards, were in unembossed, plain white frames.

Another type of cloth card was the hand-embroidered silk variety made during the period of World War I. These cards were mainly of a patriotic nature and expressed such sentiments as 'Victory and Liberty', 'Right is Might', and 'Onward to Victory'. The motifs, embroidered in colors of the Allies' flags, included regimental crests and badges. Sentimental pictures and mottoes that might express the feelings of servicemen far from loved ones were also used. These cards answered a need for the servicemen (to keep in touch with those at home without the inclination or time to write letters). 'My Dear Mother', or 'To My Sister' would

153

Main Bridge and Steele High School, Dayton.

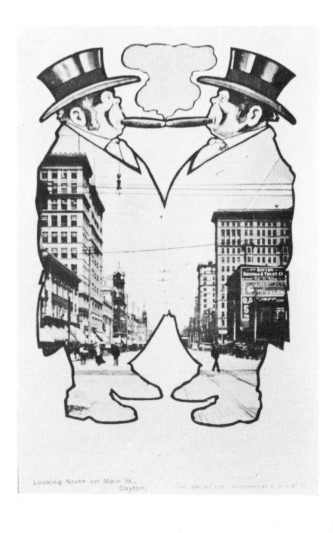

Looking North on Main St., Dayton.

154

Have a try
Don't be shy!

Top: revolving disc 'fortune-telling' card. Right: script writing applied with glue and glitter – wing of bird is three-dimensional folded tissue paper; card is double and wing pops up when opened.

Greetings from Springfield Mass

Opposite.
Top left: outline of rabbit and chicken enclose cartouches or landscapes on these Easter greeting cards. Left: unusual view cards within outlines of comic men's figures.

155

Our Christmas Song

So little holly
sprig and say:
Let all be friends
this Christmas Day.

Virginia Bioren Harrison.

A Happy New Year.

New Year's Greeting

be enough of a message to let those at home know that the young man at war was thinking of them.

These interesting and beautiful postcards of World War I first showed up in 1914 in France and they became extremely popular. The messages and pictures were embroidered on thin silk cloth ribbons in brightly colored silk thread by the women who stayed at home in France and Belgium and needed to supplement their incomes. By this period, deltiology was a universal hobby and the embroidered cards were of exceptional quality and uniqueness to appeal to those at home whose postcard albums took second place in the parlor only to the family Bible. Thousands of British, French and American soldiers were happy to let these small bits of embroidery framed in cardboard articulate their expressions of loneliness for them.

Many of these hand-made embroidered cards helped support widows and orphans of the war who did piecework on them, sometimes after finishing regular daytime jobs. The few cards of this type that were embroidered in England during the war period were made by the French refugees who lived there. The motifs

Top: pop-up children's Christmas card folds up neatly for mailing. Above: postcards with silk-finish surfaces.

**Opposite.
Top left: postcard made from a Japanese print. Top right: mechanical disc postcard; the colors and patterns change when disc is turned.
Bottom left, upper: 'We all drink beer' Swiss postcard showing people characterized as steins. Bottom left, lower: a postcard with some elements of art nouveau in the design.
Bottom right: hand-painted postcard in art style typical of 1920s.**

156

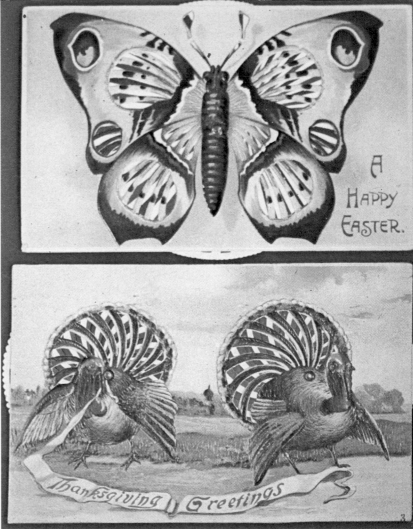

A HAPPY EASTER.

Thanksgiving Greetings

Wir trinken alle Bier - Nous buvons tous de la bière - We all drink beer.

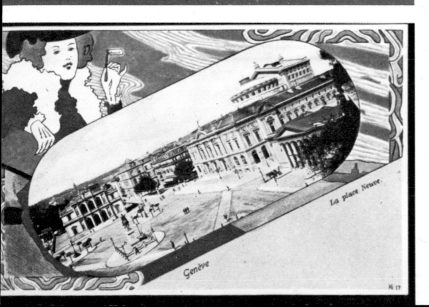

La place Neuve

Genève

PRESIDENT AND MRS. TAFT ON THEIR WAY FROM THE CAPITOL TO THE WHITE HOUSE

OHIO REGIMENT INAUGURAL PARADE

GENERAL VIEW ON PA. AVE. SHOWING THE PARADE IN THE SNOW AND SLUSH

MID SEAMEN INAUGURAL PARADE

Greetings from Newark N. J. Feb 21 1910 from Mrs Emma Cohone To Mrs A Harris

TAFT AND SHERMAN VIEWING PARADE FROM PRESIDENT'S STAND

Patent Applied for by THE PATENT ECONOMY FOLDER CO. 9-15 CLINTON ST., NEWARK, N. J.

PRESIDENT TAFT AND GOV. HUGHES REVIEWING THE 7 TH REGIMENT OF NEW YORK ON MARCH 5 TH.

PRESIDENT'S ECONOMY MAIN HOUSE LEONARD OF CLEVELAND BUILDING UNION ON PA. AVE.

7 TH REGIMENT OF NEW YORK PASSING REVIEWING STAND.

MIDDIES FROM RHODE ISLAND

SNOW SCENE OF INAUGURAL PARADE

GRANDE LOTTERIA NAZIONALE ITALIANA
PRIMO PREMIO £ 1.500.000!

Roma, 15 Luglio 1913
Serafino Bartoli
Banca d'Italia
(Italia)   Roma

Madame Nagata
Stockholm
6 Décembre 1904

RING HER UP!

Put me on a key ring,
Give me a Wedding or Phone Ring,
I Don't Care—
As long as you "Ring Me Up."

Here's To My Pipe — The Love That Is Mine
And Here's To The Girl For Whose Love I Pine
Though There's Joy In Them Both On The Dear Old Love Route
'Tis Sad For The Lover When These Two Go Out

"STRIKE A MATCH"

Art nouveau adaptation of key and pipe are unusual graphic designs.

Opposite.
Top: this elaborate folding example was souvenir of President Taft's inauguration.
Far left: double folding mailing card advertising an Italian lottery. Left: postcards with autographs of well-known people have more value to collectors.

were embroidered on long strips of silk which were then turned into the factories and starched, cut and pasted into the frames. The cards were then inserted into thin paper envelopes in which they could be mailed. Because they were hand-embroidered, no two cards of this type are exactly alike and therefore their appeal is very strong among today's collectors. The majority of the cards were sold in the early period of the war since both the manufacture and distribution were difficult once France was fighting on her own soil. However, there were many that include the flag of the United States and it becomes evident from these that many were produced through 1917–18.

Another type of novelty card that deserves some attention is the mechanical card. These have some moving part such as a disc that turns or a tab that pulls up to reveal a message or change the nature of the picture. Colorful disc cards of a kaleidoscopic nature were very popular during the height of postcard collecting as a hobby. Disc-type cards bearing revolving calendars were extremely popular.

Other novelty cards are those that have a noise-making device. These are called 'squeakers' by collectors. Others are made with a spring-type mechanism that makes it possible for a dog or other animal to have a 'wagging' tail or head. It is also assumed that many perfumed postcards were sent through the mail, but those 'smellies' of the golden age of postcards have long since lost their scent.

While discussing cards that were made to appeal to more than one of the senses, one should also mention the 'record' cards made by Raphael Tuck & Sons. This was a series of gramophone post-

159

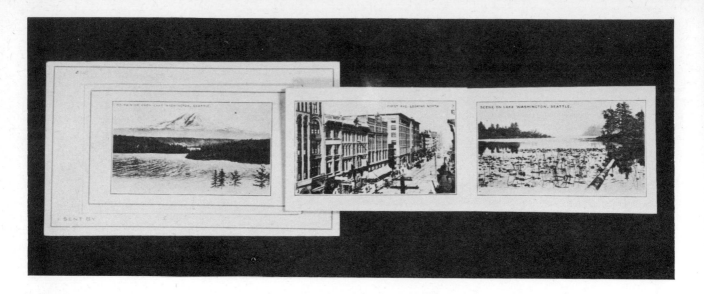

cards that had small recordings pasted on overstock postcards. The record cards were limited in number, but the cards on which they were pasted were printed in large quantities and vary considerably. One could send a friend a vocal recording of such songs as 'Auld Lang Syne', 'Annie Laurie', 'There is a Tavern in the Town', or an instrumental solo of 'D'Ya Ken John Peel?', 'Old Folks at Home' or many other favorites which were popular at the time. A birthday 'singing record' could be chosen from ten different recordings. In a patriotic vein, 'God Save the King', 'Rule Britannia', or 'When Johnny Comes Marching Home' might be torn from their postcards and played on the family gramophone. Other postcard publishers printed their recordings directly on specially prepared postcards and these could either be played with the card or cut out. At the time good quality sound was less important than the miracle of the gramophone and all records, good and bad, sounded pretty much alike on the old wind-up machines.

Top: multiple view card from Washington (state) has booklet of pictures inserted in center. Above: large letter cards of all kinds are sought by collectors; this 'name' card is 'real photograph' printed on bromide paper.

160

19

Novel Graphic and Primitive Postcards

Bookmark-size picture postcards were a novelty, but did not fit into the standard-size albums.

One type of card that is especially held in high esteem by collectors is the hold-to-light variety. The hold-to-light cards have a layer of thin colored (usually yellow) paper sandwiched between two pieces of perforated cardboard. The face of the card has a picture of a city scene, buildings, a ship or some other subject that has windows. When held to the light the windows appear lighted and the effect is always surprising and realistic.

Another type of card associated with hold-to-lights are those made with yellow or orange cellophane paper set between the two layers and these do not have to be held up for a full lighted effect.

Other cards related to the use of light to obtain their full effectiveness are those picture postcards made with foil illustrations. Light changes the appearance of the foil picture. 'Puzzle postcards' were also made with foil and on these two separate pictures are printed in alternating minute ridges of the card so that held at one angle one picture appears and held at another angle the picture changes entirely.

A metallic ink was used to print illuminated window effects on other cards. This is similar to 'day-glo' paint and when the light catches it the windows appear to be illuminated. Other cards had photographic transparencies inserted and had to be held to the light for the full effect. These examples of early transparencies are rarely found today and constitute a rather esoteric classification in deltiology.

It should be obvious by now that within the confines of a cardboard surface three-and-a-half by five-and-a-half inches an enormous variety, not only of subjects, but of printing and decorating techniques, were used to create novel cards that would have a wide appeal for collectors. The amount and variety of novelty cards that were made to satisfy collectors during the first period of avid postcard collecting makes the hobby of deltiology even more fascinating the second time round.

While one might think that the postcards mentioned in the foregoing chapter would cover just about any novel idea one might have thought of for the manufacture of picture postcards, such is not the case. There are a great many novelty cards, many of which required a lot of handwork in their manufacture or assembly or the use of an unusual material in the card itself.

Postcards were sent with coins pasted to them for luck; others had simple barometers that would change with the weather; dried

161

flowers or seaweed were pasted to postcards; mother-of-pearl letters were used; in short, any material that was fairly flat and might make it through the post.

Postcards were made of wood with designs burnt into the surface. On other wood cards the design and message might be hand-carved with a penknife. Birch bark was a favorite material for hand-made primitive cards and one unusual one is illustrated on p. 164 that has a ribbon and a dried spruce twig attached. This card was stamped and cancelled and made it half-way across the United States sixty years ago. Its inclusion in an album by the recipient has kept it in pristine condition.

Bamboo wood was another material that seemed perfect for Japanese mountain scenes. Leather cards were popular seaside and vacation spot souvenirs. Pressed Irish peat moss was made into a paper that would bring attention to that important product from Ireland. Celluloid, that forerunner of all later plastic materials, was pressed into molds with intricate designs and patterns and these cards, resembling ivory, were extremely

162

Trompe de l'oeil postcards of torn newspapers gave room for message to be written.

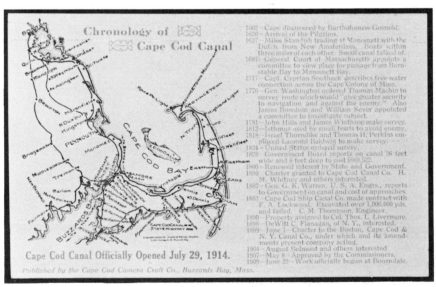

'Map' postcard of the Cape Cod Canal completed in 1914.

Opposite.
Top left: group of large number and letter cards; note that on upper three, the number of children in scene represents the number on card. Left: 'button face' hand-painted primitive postcard.

popular and have survived in excellent condition.

Double cards that folded out were made with inside centers of honeycombed and glued tissue paper sculptures. While this technique had been popular before the postcard craze as a material to be used in the design of three-dimensional greeting cards, it took some ingenuity to design postcards that could be made in a similar manner. These cards, with perforated edges that could be glued to keep the cards shut while in the mail, were opened by tearing along the perforations. Christmas trees, bells and other designs in bright colors opened up to charm the recipient.

163

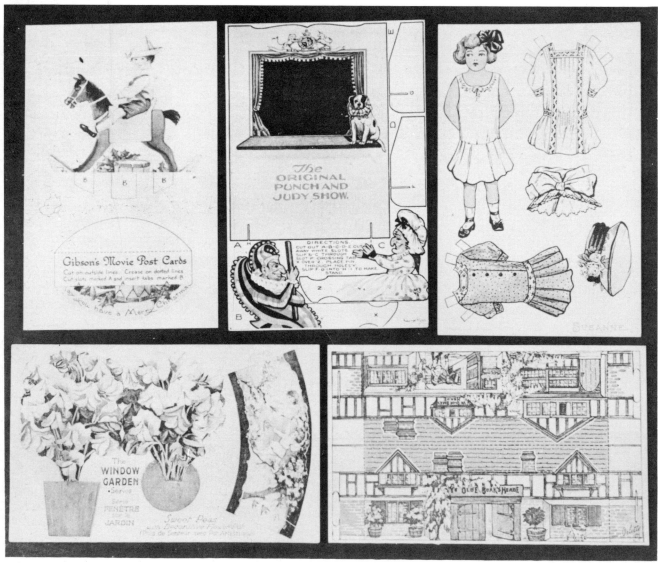

164

Above left and right, and right: a group of hand-made one-of-a-kind primitive post-cards.

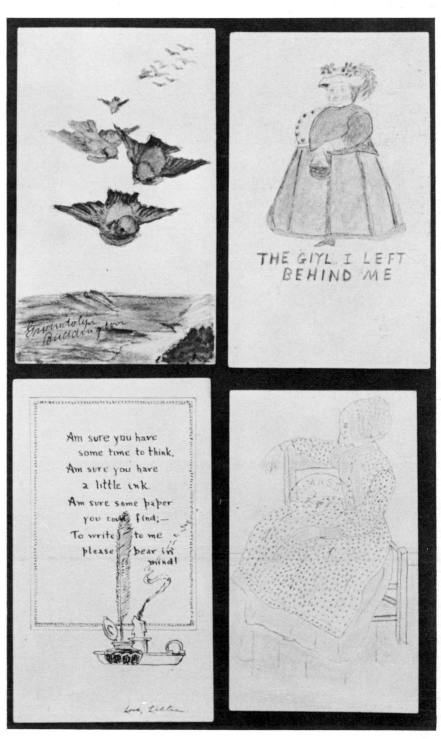

Top left: postcard made of birch bark was sent halfway across United States and obviously arrived intact. Left: children's cut-outs, games and paper dolls have not survived in quantity and are therefore desirable collector's items today.

Postcards were made in a variety of sizes and shapes, both commercially and by inventive self-made artists. Footprint shapes, the shape of a hand or mitten, box shapes and many other innovative and original designs were made.

The do-it-yourselfer had a field day in the decoration of original postcards. There were certain techniques and methods for decorating that seem to have been well known throughout the world. Buttons were pasted on cards and used as faces. The two thread holes were used for eyes and other facial features were painted on the button by hand while the rest of the body was drawn freehand by the artist. The amateur poet and writer could compose his own message and draw or paint suitable pictures to go with it. There were many such postcard primitives made and these one-of-a-kind cards are truly the gems among all examples of deltiology.

Many artistically inclined people labored over their own homemade postcards. Other artists hand-painted hundreds of postcards that were sold commercially at seaside resorts or other vacation spots. Tiny oil or tempera paintings can be found that are carefully painted works of art. Children and adults made their own cards to send to friends for their albums.

Collectors today search for graphically interesting cards where the artist's imagination led to fascinating designs of letters and numbers. Large-letter cards with photographic views inside the outlines of the letter are especially desirable to today's collectors. Letters made of flower designs and numbers, especially for New Year's greetings, made up of human figures or other unlikely graphics are typical of the search of postcard designers for the unusual and different design that would sell in quantity.

'Original' photographs, not lithographed but made on 'real bromide paper', are another collector's item today. Whether one-of-a-kind artistically painted, graphically novel, or primitive drawings done by children, all picture postcards that are novel and interesting have an important place in the field of deltiology.

The Campbell soup child with large round eyes became the trade-mark of the company and remained so for many years.

Advertisement for another American food packer, Heinz.

166

20
Advertising Postcards

It is only natural that the picture postcard should have been used throughout its history as a vehicle for advertising and propaganda, and long before its advent small colorful cards had been issued by merchants and manufacturers to advertise their goods. These were given away to customers along with colorfully printed calendars. The cards could often be packaged with the products and were usually issued with the thought that they would be welcome additions to scrapbook albums.

The most handsome of the advertising cards were made in quantity between 1880 and 1900. By 1900 the advertisers became aware of the advantage of the picture postcard over the small trade card. The cards could be mailed at little extra cost to thousands of real and potential customers. There is little doubt that the earlier advertising trade cards were the direct ancestors of the picture postcard as an advertising medium.

Early trade cards touted every product and service, from miracle bottled cures to spools of thread. Frequently stock cards, pictures of children or kittens or puppies and other popular subjects, were purchased by a store or local business and the name of that business would then be rubber-stamped on the front or back of the card.

Tobacco companies made wide use of trade cards and pretty cards were put into cigarette packages as collectible album pictures — many of these were issued in numbered series that were then collected. Allen and Ginter's cigarettes, made and packaged in Richmond, Virginia, included in their packages series of colorful cards such as 'Fans of the Period' showing pretty girls holding a variety of fans. W. Duke & Company, which called itself 'the largest cigarette manufacturers in the World', had a series of small cards called 'Fishers and Fish' and another called 'Musical Instruments'. Since only men were cigarette smokers before the turn of the century all of these cards were pictures of pretty girls, in the one case holding various kinds of just-caught fish and in the other playing a variety of instruments. These cards all had a list of the others in the series printed on the backs and they were avidly collected by the ladies who might have disapproved of the use of the 'filthy weed' but loved the cards for their albums.

As picture postcards came into common use they were used in a variety of ways for advertising purposes. Perhaps the earliest evidence of advertising on postal cards was the custom of stores or other places of business using stock postcards and rubber

167

HOOD'S SARSAPARILLA LABORATORY, LOWELL, MASS.

New, modern, factory buildings were reason for issuing advertising postcards.

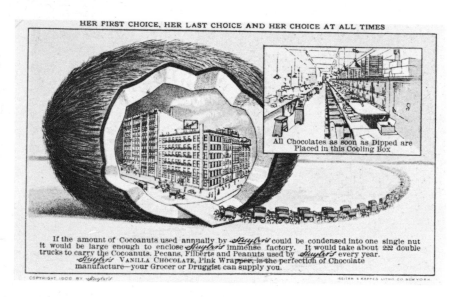

HER FIRST CHOICE, HER LAST CHOICE AND HER CHOICE AT ALL TIMES

All Chocolates as soon as Dipped are Placed in this Cooling Box

If the amount of Cocoanuts used annually by Huyler's could be condensed into one single nut it would be large enough to enclose Huyler's immense factory. It would take about 222 double trucks to carry the Cocoanuts. Pecans, Filberts and Peanuts used by Huyler's every year. Huyler's VANILLA CHOCOLATE, Pink Wrapper, is the perfection of Chocolate manufacture—your Grocer or Druggist can supply you.

A man is known by the candies he sends. Of course it's Huyler's she wants.

BOARDWALK AND BEACH SCENE.

CHOCOLATES Huyler's BON BONS ICE CREAM

Huyler's ASBURY PARK STORE ON THE BOARDWALK.

RETAIL STORES IN PRINCIPAL CITIES. SALES AGENTS EVERYWHERE.

Left and center: candy manufacturer issued these two cards to advertise its products.

stamping them with their names and addresses. Postcards were soon found to be a cheap, effective method of advertising and soon breweries, porcelain and pottery manufacturers, tea companies, furniture warehouses, clothiers, hatters and especially manufacturers of medicines and food products began to use the picture postcard as a form of advertising. Unlike the trade cards where the picture would be placed on the front and sometimes included the product, and the back of the card could be used for a

168

Advertising card for food product had all the popular elements – child, dog and cats.

Advertisement for the healthful waters of a California spa.

Far right: postcard with aircraft advertising witch hazel.

Beer companies issued many advertising postcards for their customers.

printed message, the postcards gave the sender a somewhat more limited space for his message.

It was not long before a great variety of advertising postcards were being sent through the mail and a great many novelty cards were devised that would catch the eye of the postal workers as well as the recipient. It was understood that, in the midst of the postcard collecting era, an unusual novelty stood little chance of

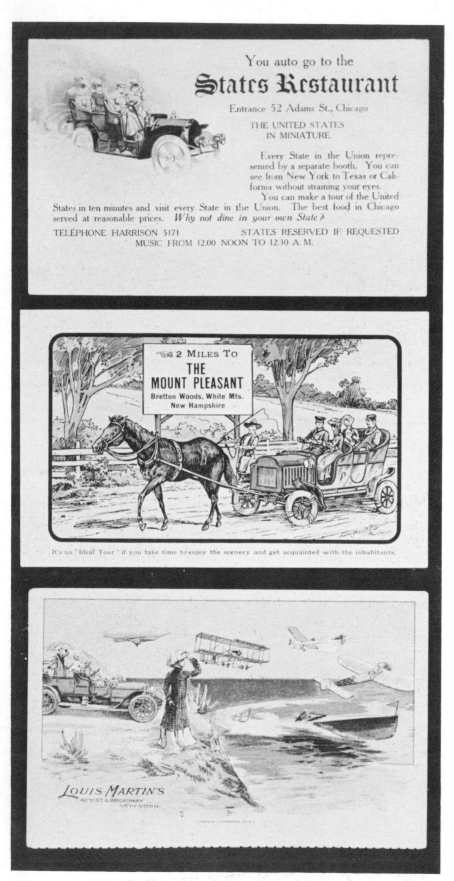

Those who collect cards of transportation subjects should not overlook advertising postcards.

170

This soldier girl in colors bright,
With bugle notes so clear,
Sounds the inspiring "Marseillaise"
That Frenchmen love to hear.
But she can play much softer tunes,
The songs both light and gay,
The songs that bring great joy to all
And drive dull care away

"Swift's Premium" Oleomargarine
Copyright 1916 Swift & Company

This sturdy little Uncle Sam
Delights to play the drum,
And soon the little patriots
From every point will come.
They'll march around as soldiers should
And rally 'round the flag.
For when the nation calls to arms
The warrior should not lag.

"Swift's Premium" Oleomargarine
Copyright 1916 Swift & Company

This pretty little Irish maid,
Dark haired, with eyes of blue,
Plays on the harp her native songs
That Erin loves so true.
The songs of love, the songs of war
Will find an answering thrill
In every brave and loyal heart
Until that heart is still.

"Swift's Premium" Oleomargarine
Copyright 1916 Swift & Company

This son of sunny Italy
Picks on the mandolin
A serenade to Juliet,
Whom he would like to win.
Though prone to songs of love and peace,
He's ready when the sounds
Of martial music loud and shrill
Through his dear land resounds.

"Swift's Premium" Oleomargarine
Copyright 1916 Swift & Company

This brave and hardy Scottish lad
Makes hill and dale resound
With "Scots Wha Hae" and
"Bonnie Doon"—
He's happy I'll be bound.
The music of the bagpipes
To the Scot is ever dear,
For when he hears its martial strains
His heart can know no fear.

"Swift's Premium" Oleomargarine
Copyright 1916 Swift & Company

The Spanish love the sweet guitar,
And Carlos here so grand
Plays all the most enchanting airs
Of that delightful land.
At evening when the work is done
The sun glows thru a haze,
The Dons and Donnas glide and whirl
Thru wild Bolero's maze.

"Swift's Premium" Oleomargarine
Copyright 1916 Swift & Company

Oleomargarine company issued series with children and flags of all nations.

THE EXHIBIT OF IDRIS & Cº Lᵀᴰ
BRITISH EMPIRE EXHIBITION - 1925

View of exhibit of advertiser at British Empire Exhibition in London in 1925.

171

being thrown away and the advertiser had the further comfort of being able to picture his card being admired in thousands of albums.

Die-cut cards with pull-up tabs could not be ignored by the recipient and one did not throw away a card that had a picture of a pedestal topped by an American eagle which, when pulled up according to directions, reveals the Statue of Liberty holding a message advertising the virtues of Eagle Pencils. Another tab card shows an American Indian woman from the back and she is carrying a papoose. When the baby's head is pulled up a rather convincing message from the Jaques Manufacturing Company entreats the viewer to try its baking powder. By the end of the nineteenth century the use of the picture postcard as an advertising medium was firmly established.

At the beginning of this century when products were being commercially packaged at a rapid rate the picture postcard was enlisted in even greater amounts to advertise them. Insurance

Juvenile postcard advertising ribbons.

172

Two postcards issued by American beer companies.

The James Hanley Brewing Company's World Famous Nine Horse Team

ONE OF THE MAGNIFICENT SIX-HORSE HITCHES OF CLYDESDALES USED BY ANHEUSER BUSCH, ST. LOUIS, BREWERS OF THE WORLD FAMOUS BUDWEISER BEER

companies could promote their rather intangible product by appealing to the public through postcards. Insurance companies understood the advantages of enlisting the aid of children in advertising and endorsing their products and one gave away colorfully printed cards with nursery rhymes. Children would, in turn, paste these into albums and few adults escaped the privilege of viewing these albums whenever they visited. The insurance companies further benefited from their gratuitousness by acquainting their potential customers at an early age with their reputation for generosity.

A new method of communication, more direct than the postcard, used the postcard as a means of advertising. Telephone companies extolled the virtues of the remarkable invention in pictures showing the instant communication between man and woman on the telephone. Even in advertising the romantic aspect of goods and services was not ignored and electric lights were advertised as being more romantic than candlelight.

Paint, lumber and sewing machines could all be advertised on picture postcards. Since a great many children kept their own albums, many cards with advertising for children's products such

173

as baby food and medicine were sent with the hope that they were pretty enough not to be thrown away, but would be carefully preserved and admired by many visitors.

In addition to the cards that were especially printed and designed with advertising, sets of previously printed cards were reissued and given as premiums. Cards with popular subjects such as children, dogs, cats, horses, famous people, etc., were

Top: an 'autograph postcard' that circulated from one recipient to another until it was filled.
Bottom: embossed and highly colored postcard has flaps that fold in and lock for mailing.

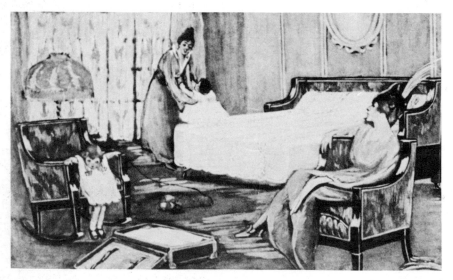

Furniture manufacturers in Grand Rapids, Michigan, showed ways in which their products could be used in room settings: note convertible sofas in lower two pictures.

174

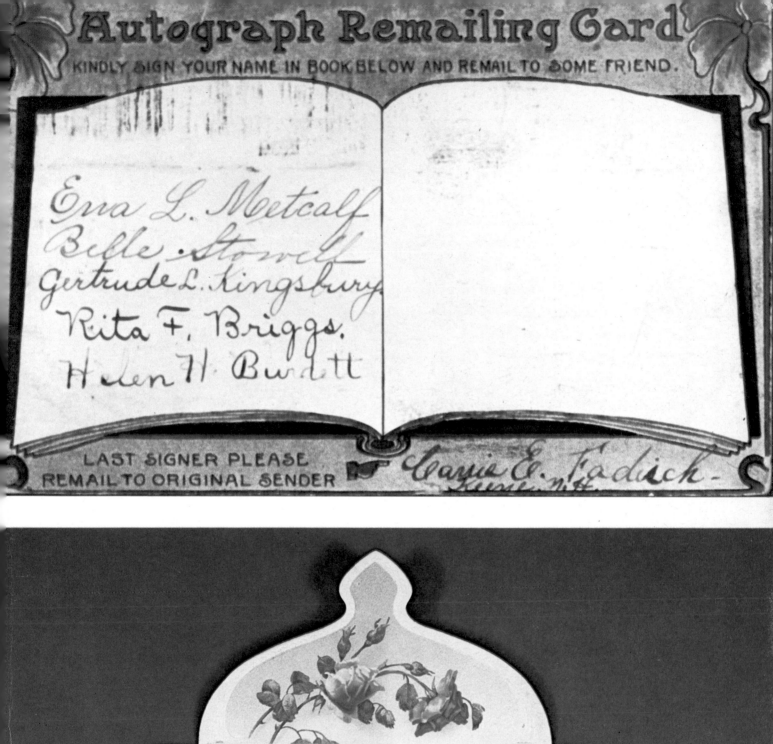

Autograph Remailing Card

KINDLY SIGN YOUR NAME IN BOOK BELOW AND REMAIL TO SOME FRIEND.

Eva L. Metcalf
Belle Stowell
Gertrude L. Kingsbury
Rita F. Briggs.
Helen H. Burtt

LAST SIGNER PLEASE
REMAIL TO ORIGINAL SENDER

Carrie E. Fadick -
Keene N.H.

Nyårs-Telegram

En välgångsönskan sänder
jag
på gamla årets
sista dag.
Blir den för Dig ett
glädjestänk
är jag belåten
med min skänk.

Gott Nytt År
tillönskas av
Wendela F.

"Lady Tatters"

"FULL INSIDE, WISH I WAS"

Shaftesbury THEATRE

Postcard probably adapted from poster design advertises play.

Right: farm machinery and poultry feed were advertised on giveaway picture postcards. Far right: British advertising card for Pears' soap.

Right: Page & Shaw chocolate was advertised on this Tuck Oilette card showing view of store front. Far right: a postcard given out to promote the use of the telephone.

simply overprinted with a few words of advertising and given away to customers. These series were as avidly collected and saved as ordinary postcards. The compulsion to complete sets or series kept customers purchasing the same product or coming back to the same store until their sets were complete. In America the face of George Washington or Abraham Lincoln on the front of a postcard used for advertising purposes was supposed to connote honesty and integrity on the part of the advertiser. In England, royalty was exploited in the same manner.

Tobacco and beer companies took advantage of the inexpensive means of advertising their products. Those who took exception to these 'symptoms of a decadent society' being sent unsolicited through the post were often mollified by the beauty of the cards and found it difficult to throw them away.

As has already been noted, steamship companies gave postcards to passengers in the hope that they would be mailed home to many parts of the world and spread the word about what a good time could be had on their cruises. One steamship company issued

177

Hotels all over the world issued advertising postcards for their clients to mail out.

Electricity was thought to need a boost on advertising postcards: 'Lovelights' series was attempt to convince public that electric light was 'romantic'.

A SHORT TIME AGO
we sent you a letter about
I C BAKING POWDER
25 ounces for 25 cts.

telling of its purity, healthfulness and merits. At that time we asked you to try it. Have you done so yet? If not, please get a can from your grocer, and if you do not find it to be all we have claimed, return it, and your money will be refunded. We want you to be the judge.

Respectfully,
JAQUES MFG. CO.
Chicago

Die-cut tab pull-out advertising postcard.

menus with detachable postcards at the top. One would suppose that the sender could write a short message on the back and send them on following a sumptuous meal and therefore, the message might contain a good word for the cuisine of that particular ship.

Railway companies sold postcards at every station and it was not unusual for passengers to jump off at stops that were just long enough and purchase a few. Restaurants also gave cards away to their clientele in the hope that they would be sent to others who would then want to try their cuisine. Raphael Tuck made railway cards for British railway companies and many hotels issued their own, most of which were printed in Germany. If the sender seemed to be enjoying himself, he might say so on the postcard and, therefore, unsolicited testimonials as to the good time and marvelous meals were circulated among friends and relatives back home.

Food products such as chocolate, cocoa, tea, baking powder, children's milk food, and other packaged foods were all advertised on picture postcards. Colognes and soaps were other products that received the benefit of colorful advertising. In short, any product that had a brand name and wide enough distribution was given the promotion on picture postcards.

A collection of advertising postcards is an interesting segment

179

IF YOU'RE ON THE SQUARE— WHY SO AM I

COPYRIGHT 1910 BY F. BLUH

LETS BURY THE HATCHET AND KISS AND MAKE UP.

COPYRIGHT 1910 BY F. BLUH.

MESSINA BEFORE THE SHOCK

KING VICTOR EMANUEL III

QUEEN HELENA

OFFICIAL
ITALIAN EARTHQUAKE RELIEF
Memorial Card
DECEMBER 28, 1908
AMERICAN ITALIAN GENERAL RELIEF COMMITTEE
WORLD BUILDING, NEW YORK

CHAIRMAN   VICE-CHAIRMAN   TREASURER

No. 33901

PRES. ROOSEVELT

W.H. TAFT, PRES. AM. RED CROSS

KING VICTOR APPALLED

MESSINA AFTER EARTHQUAKE

RED CROSS ON FIELD

180

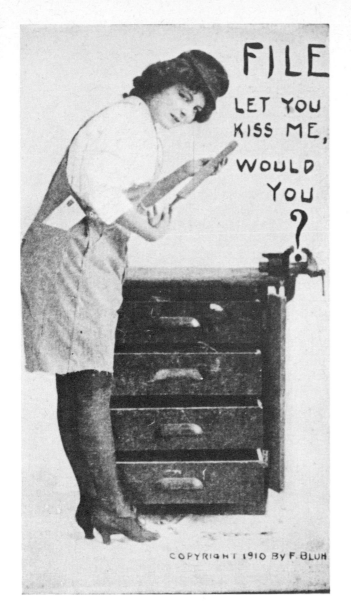

FILE LET YOU KISS ME, WOULD YOU ?

COPYRIGHT 1910 BY F. BLUH

IF YOU BRACE UP A BIT— YOU'LL WIN

COPYRIGHT 1910 BY F BLUH

Real photographic cards showing woman's legs, even from the knees down, were considered daring in 1910.

Postcard issued to raise money for Italian Earthquake Relief in 1908.

of business and advertising history of the period preceding World War I. During a period when many of our largest business conglomerates were being established, it is interesting that the medium of the picture postcard helped a lot of these companies to get started – it filled a definite need for the advertisers and could deliver a message cheaply in an effective and attractive manner. The fact that so many of these advertising cards still exist is evidence that they were thought of as attractive novelties rather than the nuisance with which advertising is viewed today.

In some cases the early advertising cards are used as adjunctive material for collections of objects other than postcards. The American bottle collector, for instance, searches for advertisements of products that were packaged in glass such as medicines and baby food products. Soft drink manufacturers used the picture postcard for early advertising as did dairies and beer companies. These cards are all of interest to bottle collectors who can sometimes identify the use of old bottles by this method.

Collectors of pottery and porcelain search for advertisements on postcards that might help identify as to maker and style certain objects that they might own. Railroad buffs can hardly find a better record of what the early railways, the stations and

181

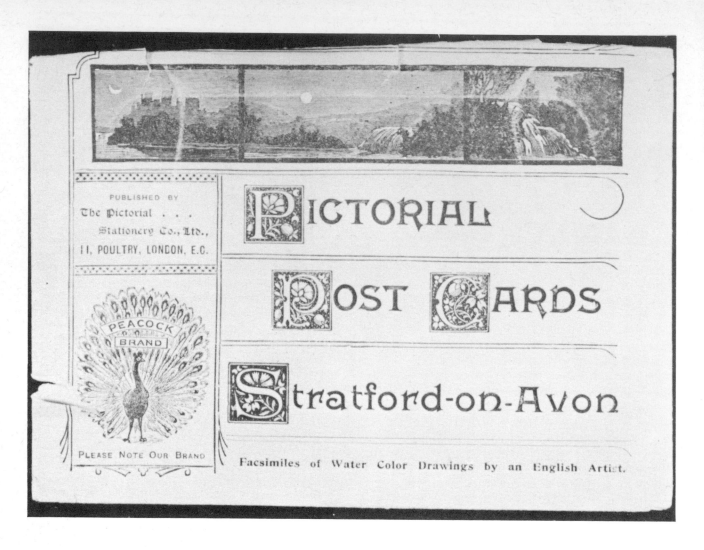

PUBLISHED BY
The Pictorial . . .
Stationery Co., Ltd.,
11, POULTRY, LONDON, E.C.

PEACOCK BRAND

PLEASE NOTE OUR BRAND

PICTORIAL POST CARDS Stratford-on-Avon

Facsimiles of Water Color Drawings by an English Artist.

engines looked like than the cards printed by Raphael Tuck and others. Historians can find a great deal of business history documented on picture postcards that were especially printed as advertising aids. Similarly, both manufacturers and retailers that have long been out of business can be documented by the study of their advertising using the same medium. The great tourist hotels and spas of pre-World War I days, long since torn down, can be studied on the picture postcards that were sent out or given to clients. Advertising for products that were newly invented at the turn of the century such as a 'revolutionary ice-cream maker' or 'leak-proof fountain pens' give us a pictorial record of some of these inventions.

Many advertisers sent out calendar cards at Christmas time in the hope that the cards would be kept in a purse or pocket and referred to all year. Special amusing cards were made up for traveling salesmen so that they could let their clients know that they would be calling at a particular time in the future. One such card showing a man in a cart with a runaway horse and his sample goods flying off the back is an early form of a 'write-away' card with the printed message, 'Even if I should miss the train I will surely be in to see you on or about . . .' A blank was left for the time to be filled in and a signature that went over the printed name of the company being represented. Postal deliveries were swift, dependable and frequent in those days and the salesman could be assured that his client would receive his message in plenty of time. For a penny stamp the salesman and the company that he worked for could establish a relationship with the client that might lead to a big order.

Sets of pictorial postcards came in envelopes such as the one pictured here: often envelopes advertised other new series issued by publisher.

182

21

Care and Repair of Old Postcards

In comparison to its two related hobbies, coin and stamp collecting, the collecting of picture postcards has some advantages. Prices for the most rare postcards are nowhere near the amount one must pay for rare coins or stamps. Unlike coins, there is no intrinsically valuable material involved and the possibilities of theft are less. Stamp collections can be extremely valuable or worth little, depending upon completeness, rarity and other factors. However, unlike coins or stamps, picture postcards require a little more space for storage. They also require a little care and some need a small amount of repair.

Experienced deltiologists search for cards in pristine or 'mint' condition, but the more rare cards are not always available in an unused state. When one comes by an old album full of good cards it is heartbreaking to find that the original collector has pasted them to the pages. This sometimes can mean that the cards are beyond help. However, if the paper in the album is of the thin, manilla type, most cards will not suffer from being soaked in warm water until the album paper is thoroughly wet. It can then be rubbed off by gently rolling the thumb over the surface of the card. When glued to heavier paper, it is sometimes difficult to remove the cards by soaking since the prolonged soaking needed to wet the heavy paper thoroughly enough to remove it can also be damaging to the card itself. Once the card has been cleaned off and all possible traces of paste or glue removed, it should be placed between layers of paper towels and a weight placed on it until it is dry. This is to prevent warping. Obviously, the best way to purchase old cards is in an album that was properly made for postcards with slits for corner insertions.

The collector should remember that the more times a postcard is removed and replaced in corner slits or embossed stick-on corner holders such as those made for photograph albums, the more possibility there is of tearing or chipping the corners. This is the damage most commonly found on old postcards. Since many of the postcards that are most valuable are old and rather thick, many of them have become somewhat brittle with age and should be handled as little as possible.

The best method for storing postcards, especially for the new collector who would prefer to invest his money in cards rather than storage material, is to find the proper size shoe boxes and use those. These will keep the cards in decent order and condition. Two-drawer five-inch by six-inch metal card files are used by more experienced deltiologists whose collections warrant careful cataloging and care. These can be added to, one unit at a time, as one's collection grows. An alternative is to use clear plastic shoe-boxes, which stack well and are somewhat less expensive. A disadvantage to shoe-boxes for the large collection is that they only open from the top and if stacked this becomes an inconvenience. Cardboard shoe-boxes can be painted or covered with wallpaper or plasticised sticky patterned paper for a uniform and attractive appearance.

While only a few short years ago old postcard albums (and their contents) could be purchased at auction for very little money, the growth of picture postcard collecting as a hobby has raised the prices for these attractive books. Made at the turn of the century in Europe and America to satisfy the needs of the thousands of collectors of that period, many of these albums have covers decorated in *art nouveau* style and these are in demand, not only by card collectors, but by those who enjoy the art style. Few of these old albums are usable today. The paper pages have become brittle and the slits that hold the corners of the cards more often than not tear at the removal of the cards. The albums are worth owning as adjunctive material to picture postcard collections. They are purchased today, not so much as storage for card collections, but for their value as period art. Some of the stamped cover designs are hand-painted and others are made of tooled leather.

New, more practical, albums are currently being made. These are loose-leaf binders and each leaf will hold up to six cards in clear plastic pages. Although somewhat expensive, the new albums are an ideal way to store the better cards, those that are worth the extra investment to insure that they are not damaged from exposure to moisture, dirt and handling.

Glassine envelopes of postcard size are made for collectors and are inexpensive covers for cards filed in boxes or metal file drawers. One can see through them and identify and admire cards without damaging them. At a very low price apiece the envelopes are a good investment for serious collectors of good old cards. While the envelopes are 50 per cent more expensive than some of the postcards themselves were when new, many of the cards they will protect are now worth so much more than their original cost, and they are worth the extra investment to keep them in good condition as values rise.

Considering the ephemeral qualities of old postcards it is remarkable that so many can be found with no damage. One might expect this of unused cards that have been protected for seventy-five years in an album. However, it is not unusual to find used cards that have been written on, gone through the post and cancellation and even crossed oceans that look like new today. Many of these were printed on good quality cardboard. Some of the fancy cards, such as the French wartime silk embroidered cards, were mailed in special envelopes and therefore had some protection. The two most common damages found on old cards are dirty surfaces and dog-eared corners. Often the damage to the corners came about from early collectors attempting to force the cards into the page slits made to hold them in albums. When sticky corners were used to hold the cards, these often were damaging to the cards, especially if they had been removed and replaced. These corners were used when ordinary scrapbooks rather than postcard albums were used to house the collection. Sometimes collectors interspersed postcards with

Well-designed French art nouveau postcard in orange and brown with gold.

snapshots or calendar pictures and trade cards. Anything printed in color was 'collectible' and many postcards were simply glued into an album.

One cannot do too much about repairing dog-eared corners. If the corners are torn and none of the paper or surface coating missing, a small bit of white glue can be used to repair them. However, this is only effective when there is a clean tear with all parts of the card intact. The only time to make any investment in a dog-eared card is when it is needed to fill in a series, but one should discard it when a cleaner specimen is found.

Dirt can be removed safely from surfaces of cards by the use of a soft rubber eraser. More stubborn dirt can sometimes be removed by gently wiping the surface with a slightly damp cloth and drying immediately with a dry one. Cotton wool can also be used for this purpose. If the card is worthless in its present condition there is little to be lost by attempting to restore it to its original condition. Most good quality cards will not suffer from this sort of treatment. Naturally, any card with hand painting or

185

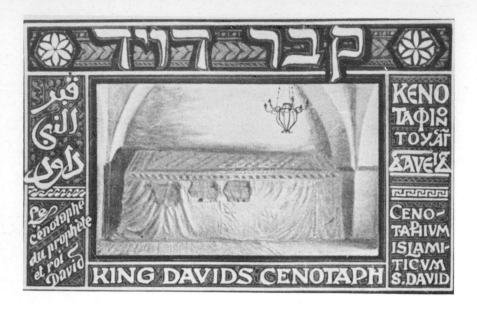

Multi-lingual postcard was souvenir from the Holy Land.

applied material such as cloth or glitter should not be treated in this manner.

Damage to a postcard devalues it considerably. However, those that might be found to have a tear, if they are scarce, should be preserved. Further damage can be prevented by the application of sticky clear tape to the address side of the postcard. Regardless of the resale value of a damaged card, the rare ones should be preserved since they add something to the complete story of picture postcards and therefore are of historical value to deltiologists. For instance, no Clapsaddle card, regardless of condition, should be disposed of until it has been checked against the existing checklists to make sure that others like it have been documented.

Although the truly serious collectors consider any method of displaying picture postcards in a manner that might destroy their condition to be almost bordering on the sacrilegious, old postcards can be very decorative when matted and framed either singly or in groups. Modern collectors need not go to lengths of the earlier collectors who decorated everything from lampshades to workbaskets with picture postcards. Framing the cards will not damage them and some of the more colorful ones make very handsome framed pictures. Many of the more commonly found cards that are nevertheless beautifully colored have been used consistently throughout this century for decoupage decoration.

For display at exhibits there are accordion-folded clear plastic sleeves made that will protect your cards. When picture postcards are to be mounted on a board for exhibit, use photographer's embossed glued corners to hold them. The corners are slipped onto the card *before* the card is mounted. In this manner the card won't have to be bent to force it into that fourth corner. Also, although all postcards of regular size appear to be uniform, there is really a great variation in the sizes and once the corners have been stuck on the boards, few of the cards will be interchangeable.

Card collections in storage should be checked every so often, depending upon the area in which one lives. Dampness can be damaging to cardboard. Also, there are some insects indigenous to various parts of the world that thrive on paper. If silverfish (of the termite family) are common in your area make certain that your cards are well protected in glassine or cellophane envelopes and metal files.

186

22

About Value

Just as it is with any commodity that is bought, sold or traded, picture postcards will find their own monetary level according to the rule of supply and demand. Although thousands of old and beautifully lithographed picture postcards can still be purchased on both sides of the Atlantic for a penny apiece, there are many others that have soared in price during the current postcard collecting boom. Naturally, those that are most wanted and that are rarely found today are the most expensive. Prices rise considerably as new research is done and attention is brought to certain artists, publishers or types of cards.

Certain view cards can be more valuable than others. If an early view card has pictures of early automobile models in it or one of the less commonly found post offices or railway stations it will be of increased value to many collectors who specialise in these categories. Postcards from the Boer War or World War I are worth many times their original cost.

Certain artist-signed postcards have increased tremendously in value in the past ten years even though there should be no shortage of these. When the postcard publishers had a popular artist working for them they printed millions of just one of his works. There are regional preferences for artist-signed cards as well. In Great Britain, Asti, Kirchner, Louis Wain, Caton Woodville and Ethel Parkinson are popular. American deltiologists look for Frances Brundage, Ellen H. Clapsaddle and Rose O'Neill signed cards. Harry Payne's cards are popular on both sides of the ocean since he designed so many with American scenes and motifs. All artist-signed cards, especially those for which check lists have been written and published, will go up in value. *Art nouveau* style cards, especially those designed by Mucha, are at present more popular in England but will probably be in high demand in the United States soon.

Many of the novelty cards illustrated here have become rare, either due to the fragile nature of the materials from which they were made, or because few of each kind were made to begin with. Postcards made of unusual material such as wood, bark or peat are wanted by collectors and are, therefore, apt to cost more than the average. Any cards that were made wholly or in part by hand will have an increasing value, as well they should. The Stevensgraphs and other woven silk cards, especially 'Fab' cards, are also in short supply due to the fact that these are collected by people whose first interest is not postcards, but embroidery and the decorative arts.

Postcards that were made to be cut up or parts of them used in some way obviously didn't survive in sufficient quantity to satisfy today's collectors, and therefore these have become scarce and expensive. For instance, jigsaw puzzle cards were easily lost or

187

thrown away once the puzzle had been taken apart and put together once or twice. There was no place for such a postcard in the albums that preserved so many other examples. Children's cut-outs and paper dolls did not survive in quantity for obvious reasons. Installment cards are rarely found with the entire set intact. Sets of these have added value when they are found in good condition.

The earliest postcards of any country are in strong demand, not only by deltiologists, but by the many postal history buffs. Therefore, the Columbian Exhibition postal cards, the British Eddystone Lighthouse and the earliest Eiffel Tower cards are in strong demand and short supply and, therefore, extremely expensive.

Any picture postcards with portraits of royalty, statesmen or politicians, including American political campaign items, are collected by historians and there are so many of these specialist collectors that many of the cards are apt to be quite expensive. For instance, there are thousands of collectors in the United States who search for picture postcards bearing reference to Abraham Lincoln and George Washington and the most difficult cards to find in these categories are the ones that will obviously cost more. Since neither of these American presidents lived when postcards were being produced it might do well for historians to collect the many cards made for the presidents that were contemporary with the postcard craze. As time goes on these will undoubtedly have more value than cards made to commemorate the death, birth and presidency of the two most popular presidents.

When certain postcards are desired as related material to hobbies other than postcard collecting, the demand is higher and, therefore, the prices will rise. For instance, numismatists and philatelists search for the coin and stamp cards previously described and illustrated. This makes the cards difficult to find. In addition, stamp and coin collectors are used to paying higher prices for additions to their collections and will, therefore, outbid a postcard collector who might want just one or two Ottmar Zieher cards for his collection. This is also true of autograph collectors who purchase lots of postcards in the hope that they will come across one signed by a famous person. Unusual cancellations and certain stamps add value to postcards from the beginning of this century.

If one collects postcards with pictures of dirigibles, early flying machines or railway trains he is already aware that the demand is high and that he will have to pay more for sharing interests similar to many other deltiologists. Balloons are another category that has many devotees.

Regional view cards that are wanted by many members in one location are apt to increase in value as the supply of interesting old cards dwindles. Postcard collectors tend to become somewhat chauvinistic concerning their place of birth, their old school, or local main streets. If the new collector picks views of a locality that is not close to where he lives he may find that his chances for increasing his specialist collection can grow for very little investment.

Picture postcards of exceptional graphic quality such as Tuck's Limited Edition cards, art gallery reproductions published by Nister, Misch & Company or Stengel and interesting hand-painted picture postcards (especially if these are signed by the artist) are always going to demand higher prices. Cards with

188

applied material that had to be made wholly or in part by hand (such as the decoupage variety made from cancelled stamps), button faces, cards with applied hair, fur or other material, will become more valuable with time.

Certain publishers such as Tuck of England or Detroit or International Art of the United States are already in high demand and eventually stock will run low and prices increase on all cards from the better publishers.

Postcards that are interesting from a photographic history point of view, such as the early Detroits or those that have an exceptional graphic quality typical of the time in which the cards were printed, will also continue to increase in value. Among them are the heavily embossed papier maché cards with airbrush painting, large-letter cards, large-date cards, crested cards and many others.

One should always keep in mind that postcards were issued in sets for the early collectors, and when sets can be found intact they are always worth more than if the cards are purchased singly. This is also true of specialised collections. Once a collector has amassed several thousand cards in a single category he has increased his overall investment many times. If the collection is broken up when it is sold, it is again decreased.

To get a clear idea of the relative value of old picture postcards one can go to the auction lists published frequently in some of the postcard club periodicals listed in the Bibliography. Unlike other collectible old items, many beautiful picture postcards can still be purchased for just a few pennies. What one collects will depend to some degree on what one can afford. Any experienced deltiologist has a rather clear idea of what certain cards in his specialty will cost.

Because the supply of most cards that are collected is still ample, one can always hope for that special 'find' that most collectors watch for; this is the old album, straight from someone's attic, that has not been opened in fifty years. If the album dates from the period before World War I, some of the cards will have value. Since many postcard collectors are also dealers (what other way is there to get rid of unwanted cards?) most experienced collectors know something about relative values.

There is only one thing that is certain about the prices of most beautiful old picture postcards. They will consistently increase in value as more and more members are added to the rosters of postcard collectors' clubs and the supply of the most desirable issues becomes shorter. Postcard collecting is still a hobby one can indulge in without spending a fortune and the rewards in knowledge and enjoyment are well worth any investment.

In terms of increase in value from their original cost when new, picture postcards have the distinction of having already, as a collector's item, increased the most, in terms of percentage, of any collector's category today. Objects that originally sold for as little as a penny apiece are now worth many times that amount, but still can be purchased for very little investment. It is to be hoped that the recent attention that is being brought to picture postcards made before World War I will not price those objects out of the reach of the thousands who have once again discovered the joys of collecting them. One should take a second look at the albums that have been stored away in the attic since grandmother passed away to discover a new world of collecting that most perfectly gives us a picture of the old world.

Acknowledgments

I am most grateful to Mrs Ruth MacCallum who was extremely generous in sharing her knowledge and her library on postcards with me. Without her help this book could not have been written. The collection of Mrs MacCallum and her husband, George, is on display at the Post Card Museum in Canaan, Connecticut. Mr and Mrs MacCallum's comprehensive and carefully chosen collection were made available to us for photographing and study.

I would also like to thank Mr and Mrs Melvin S. Sutton and Mr William H. Watkins, Director of the Mattatuck Museum in Waterbury, Connecticut, for their help in loaning postcards for study and photographing.

Bibliography

Alderson, F. *The Comic Postcard in English Life.* David and Charles. Devon, 1969.

Burdick, J. R. *Pioneer Postcards.* Nostalgia Press. New York, 1956.

Carline, Richard. *Pictures in the Post.* Gordon Fraser. Bedford, 1959.

Corson, Walter C. *Publisher's Trademarks Identified.* Better Postcard Collectors' Club. Folsom, Pa., 1962.

Hill, C. W. *Discovering Picture Postcards.* Deltiologists of America. Folsom, Pa., 1970.

Holt, Toni and Valmai. *Picture Postcards of the Golden Age : a Collector's Guide.* Deltiologists of America. Folsom, Pa., 1971.

Kaduck, John M. *Mail Memories.* 'Memories', Box 02152, Cleveland, Ohio, 1971.

Lowe, James L. *Bibliography of Postcard Literature.* Folsom, Pa., 1969.

Peterson, William J. *The Palimpsest.* Volume XLVIII, No. 12. December, 1967. (Journal of the State Historical Society of Iowa.)

Staff, Frank. *The Picture Postcard and its Origins.* Frederick A. Praeger. New York, 1966.

Organs of postcard collecting organisations used:

Centennial of the Post Card, Werner Von Boltenstern, Co-ordinator. Los Angeles, California, 1969–70.

Deltiology. Deltiologists of America. Folsom, Pa.

The Lone Star Bulletin. Lone Star Post Card Collectors' Club. Waco, Texas.

Monthly Bulletin of the Metropolitan Post Card Collectors Club. Metropolitan Post Card Collectors Club. New York.

Po Cax-71. First annual South Jersey Post Card Exhibition. Mt. Ephraim, New Jersey.

The Postcard Collector. The Southern California Postcard Club. Los Angeles, California.

The Post Card Traveler. An independent postcard publication. Edited by Steve and Kay Staruck. Garwood, New Jersey.

What Cheer News. Rhode Island Post Card Club. Providence, R.I.

Index